Praise for *Real Leaders Don't Boss*

"In college athletics, where building our brand is so important, the right kind of leadership is critical to long-term success. Ritch Eich knows this, and understands the complicated process that results in true leadership. Ritch has deep leadership knowledge and experience, and *Real Leaders Don't Boss* will provide valuable information to all who want to further develop their leadership skills."

—David Brandon, director of athletics, The University of Michigan, and former chairman and CEO, Domino's Pizza

"Ritch Eich is a leader's leader, with a magical ability to turn the impossible into the possible. He brings to whatever he does exceptional experience, know-how, enthusiasm, and connections. Now, with his book, his unique transformational approach to leadership will be available to everyone."

—William Kearney, senior vice president, Merrill Lynch

"Ritch Eich's leadership style is part Warren Bennis and Max Depree, part John Greenleaf and Peter Drucker, and part Jackie Robinson and Colin Powell. Ritch is a change agent and has worked tirelessly to transform the management practices and processes he inherited in each of his positions of increasing responsibility. As a leadership and management consultant, Ritch is continuing to share 'best practices' from the leadership field."

—Steve Grafton, president and CEO, The University of Michigan Alumni Association

D0878417

"Whether you're a new manager or a new executive, Ritch Eich delivers an exceptionally useful pathway to follow for success. Ritch is highly accomplished, incredibly disciplined, and leads by example and with humor and with grace. Don't go to your next staff meeting without reading his book first!"

—Mary D. Olson, general manager, KCLU Radio, NPR

"No matter what stage you are at in your career, *Real Leaders Don't Boss* will help you get to the next level. Ritch's vast experience in healthcare and higher education shine through and his insight is refreshing. If you want to be a better leader yourself, or if you want to help others develop their leadership skills, read and share this book."

—Ora Hirsch Pescovitz, MD, executive vice president for Medical Affairs University of Michigan, and CEO, University of Michigan Health System

"The essence of Ritch Eich's approach is to listen, analyze, and communicate. His intellect and training, buttressed by his fundamental instincts, are valuable assets in any problem-solving environment."

—Eugene A. Bauer, MD, former CEO, Stanford University Medical Center, and former dean, Stanford University School of Medicine

"Books and articles about leadership are not scarce. Insightful books drawn from career-long, successful, hands-on experience are. Ritch Eich brings that experience to his valuable discussion of traits and qualities—some learned, some innate—possessed by the best leaders. His book is careful in describing the difference between leading and managing, a chasm he so clearly understands from his own successful careers."

—Jim Finkelstein, Chief of Information, Navy Department, Pentagon, Rear Admiral, U.S. Navy (Ret.)

"Ritch Eich has captured the essence of leadership in his book, *Real Leaders Don't Boss.* People may gain wealth or promotions by the sheer power of their personality and desire, however the success of the organization fades as soon as they leave and they usually leave untold numbers of casualties in their wake. Real leaders know their trade as well, but they are guided by virtues such as fortitude and temperance. They value those that work for them. They also challenge and mentor them. Real leaders are comfortable in their own skin which in turn develops the character of those who work for them."

—Major General Leslie M. Palm, USMC (Ret.), president and CEO, Marine Corps Association & Foundation (Ret.)

"Ritch has a strong passion for the principles, morals, and ethics that make great leaders. In a world where it's increasingly difficult to know who to trust, you can trust Ritch."

—Ross K. Goldberg, president, Kevin/Ross Public Relations and co-founder, Society for Healthcare Strategy and Market Development

"Readers will learn from bosses who have led important organizations to places worthy of the deep personal commitment of those who have followed them."

—Dan Beckham, president, The Beckham Company

"*Real Leaders Don't Boss*—a 'must read.' Ritch has continued his fervent commitment to share with university students all the leadership skills he has mastered throughout his very successful career."

—Harold Edwards, president and CEO, Limoneira Company

"Most books on leadership are not worth reading because they are long on the theory of leadership, but miss the heart of leadership. *Real Leaders Don't Boss* is an important exception. If you are interested in the 'whys' and 'hows' of leadership, get a copy, snag a couple of hours to read it, and you will have the insights you need to be the leader you have always wanted to be."

—Robert A. Sevier, PhD, senior vice president, Stamats, Inc.

REAL LEADERS DON'T BOSS

Inspire, Motivate, and Earn Respect From Employees and Watch Your Organization Soar

By Ritch K. Eich, PhD

Pompton Plains, NJ

REAL LEADERS DON'T BOSS
TYPESET BY DIANA GHAZZAWI
Cover design by Rob Johnson, Toprotype
Printed in the U.S.A.

To order this title, please call toll-free 1-800-CAREER-1 (NJ and Canada: 201-848-0310) to order using VISA or MasterCard, or for fur-ther information on books from Career Press.

The Career Press, Inc.
220 West Parkway, Unit 12
Pompton Plains, NJ 07444
www.careerpress.com

Library of Congress Cataloging-in-Publication Data
Eich, Ritch K.
    Real leaders don't boss : inspire, motivate, and earn respect from employees and watch your organization soar / by Ritch K. Eich.
        p. cm.
    Includes bibliographical references and index.
    ISBN 978-1-60163-186-2 -- ISBN 978-1-60163-640-9 (ebook)
    1. Leadership. 2. Interpersonal communication. 3. Employee motivation. I. Title.
HD57.7.E373 2012
658.4'092--dc23

2011037718

Dedication

This book is dedicated to my grandfather, Harvey D. Eich, longtime community leader, teacher, principal, and four-term treasurer of Yuba County, California, and to my grandmother, "Mama Dean."

To my parents, Wilton and Joanne Eich, who provided an abundance of love and devotion, and by their example instilled in me the importance of service to others.

To my brother, Ron, a natural leader whose scholarship, sense of humor, business acumen, and tireless community leadership from Cal Berkeley to IBM to Mendocino, who, along with his wife, Joan Stiles Eich, and their family, were an inspiration to me.

To my sister, Kathleen Eich McKinnie, her husband "Mac," and family, for their sincere interest in my career.

To my wife's parents, Edward and Verla Cummings, for their intellectual stimulus and fascinating discussions that I will always treasure.

To my wife's sisters and their husbands, Cecily and Ralph Wood, and Kathy and Fran Larsen, for their enduring friendship and companionship.

And, finally, to my wife, Joan Taylor Cummings Eich, my partner and best friend, and to our sons, Geoff and Ted, and their spouses, Nancy and Mary, and our grandchildren, Taylor Sun, John Patrick, Carter Jameson, and Caroline Elizabeth, whose continuing encouragement, support, and legion of leadership lessons are invaluable to me.

Thank you!

Acknowledgments

Many very talented people contributed mightily to this book in countless ways, including Michael Lynn Adams; Larry Ames; Ken Beachler; R. Duke Blackwood (director, Ronald Reagan Presidential Library); Mike Bradbury, JD; David Brandon; Eugene A. Bauer, MD; John Chamberlain; Dr. Jack M. Christ; Mike Craft; Scott Dennis and his reference desk colleagues (University of Michigan Libraries); Rich DeVos; Henry Dubroff; Joe Dulin; Don Dupuis; Harold Edwards; Tim Elson (Buchanan Group); Lisa Evans; RADM Jim Finkelstein, USN (Ret.); Jeff Folks; Steve Grafton; Ross Goldberg; Erik Hagen; Norm Hartman; Mark Helmke; Howard S. "Howdy" Holmes; Bill Kearney; Carol Keochekian; Emily Krueger; U.S. Senator Richard G. Lugar; Mike McCurry; Bruce McRoy, JD; Jan Mendenhall; John T. Moore; Mary Olson; Lance Orozco; Maj. Gen. Les Palm, USMC (Ret.); Tony Pals; Ora Hirsch Pescovitz, MD; Marianne Ratcliff; Dean Rennell (president, Wells Fargo, Arizona Region); Jim Rondeau; Richard Schreiner, MD; Lisa Cuevas Shaw; Blaise Simqu; Laura M. Smith; Don Steel; Raymond Sun; John Ullmen; Marlize van Romburgh; Michele von Dambrowski; Patti Waid; Clifton R. Wharton, Jr., PhD; and Mrs. Dolores D. Wharton.

They were unselfish with their time, unvarnished yet always thoughtful in their critiques, passionate about the subject, demonstrably assertive in urging me to move forward in this undertaking, or contributed in other important ways. I am deeply indebted to all of them and sincerely hope I didn't overlook anyone. If I did, I apologize profusely.

I have been privileged to work with and for many highly successful leaders, as well as several remarkably skilled teams of professionals in healthcare, higher education, the U.S. Navy and Marines, and elsewhere, and humbled by numerous opportunities to observe, meet, and interact with many of the best and brightest in our nation's businesses.

Myriad organizations have published my writing, and I wish to publicly thank several in particular for their support and professional courtesy in this work. They include *Communication Quarterly*; *Costco Connection*; the *Los Angeles Business Journal*; the *Los Angeles Daily News*; *Marine Corps Gazette*; *Miller-McCune Magazine*; *Modern Healthcare*; *Pacific Coast Business Times*; *Payers & Providers*; *Sales and Service Excellence*; *Santa Barbara News Press*; *Stanford University Report*; *Strategic Health Care Marketing*; *Thousand Oaks ACORN*; *Trusteeship Magazine* and *AGB*, the U.S. Naval Institute and *Proceedings* magazine; and the *Ventura County Star*, among many others.

Every author of every book or article I've read on this fascinating topic has taught me something of value. To Dan Beckham, Warren Bennis, Ram Charan, Jim Collins, Chris Denove, Ross Goldberg, John Kotter, James Kouzes, Larry Lauer, Jeffrey Pfeffer, Barry Posner, J.D. Power IV, Charles O'Reilly, Robert Sevier, Robert Sutton, RADM William Thompson USN (Ret.), Noel Tichy, and other distinguished authors, I ask that you keep writing to further deepen our understanding of the leadership skills required in a dynamically changing world.

A very special, heartfelt expression of my deepest gratitude is extended to Ross Goldberg, president of Kevin/Ross Public

Relations, for his enduring friendship, wonderful tutelage, and good judgment. His writing is exemplary, and his wise, savvy, and candid counsel is irreplaceable.

I also wish to express my sincere thanks to the superb team at my publishing house, Career Press, for their faith in me, their expertise, and their willingness to always go the extra mile in coming to my rescue when I required their assistance: Michael Pye, Jeff Piasky, Adam Schwartz, Laurie Kelly-Pye, Kirsten Dalley, and Diana Ghazzawi. And last but hardly least, I take my hat off to my literary colleagues, mentors, and editors par excellence Cynthia Zigmund of Second City Publishing Services, Susan J. Marks, and Laura M. Smith for their invaluable guidance, incomparable knowledge, and literary mastery. They are the best!

The first guy through a wall always gets bloody...

—Prophetic words spoken to me by
my company commander,
boot camp, Recruit Training Command,
Naval Training Center,
Great Lakes, Illinois,
a very cold December 1968

Contents

Foreword

I've read many leadership books and must say that *Real Leaders Don't Boss* was a refreshing and recommendable read that offers inspiring insights on being a leader at any level.

Ritch Eich draws on his vast and diverse experiences in agriculture, the military, higher education, healthcare, business, and consulting to thoughtfully and skillfully provide readers with no-nonsense, practical "takeaways" that can be applied in any organization (no matter what size) and used by any professional (no matter what role).

This is not just a book for the business or medical student or the corporate leader. There are valuable lessons for anyone in the workplace who wants to better understand what his or her contribution means and how to achieve great results.

Real Leaders Don't Boss is easy to read, as well as a book you will want to keep handy so you can refer to it time and again.

It has been my good fortune to know Ritch for several years, beginning when we worked together at Riley Hospital for Children in Indianapolis and now as we both have roles with the University of Michigan. I continue to be greatly impressed by him and especially by his extraordinary ability to develop young leaders.

As a board member of the Alumni Association of the University of Michigan, Ritch serves more than 525,000 living alumni around the world. He understands that leadership is not some sort of mathematical formula, but rather an art that can be learned experientially.

No matter what stage you are in your career, this book will help you get to the next level. If you want to be a better leader yourself, or if you want to help others develop their leadership skills, read and share this book.

—Ora Hirsch Pescovitz, MD, executive vice president for Medical Affairs University of Michigan, and CEO, University of Michigan Health System

Introduction

Leadership is not a gimmick. It does not come from weekend seminars or strictly from guidebooks. A "Stalinesque" approach to bossing employees and peers won't net solid results either, at work or in life. Real and effective leaders today—whether they lead from the C-suite (a term commonly used to refer to a company's senior executives), the assembly line, the PTO, or in personal relationships—quietly and consistently rely instead on the Eight Essentials of Effective Leadership, which will be discussed in this book.

True leaders know how to make ethical judgments in the face of real-world challenges. They recognize what it takes to win loyalty and respect, to motivate through passion, to develop positive relationships, to enhance open communication, and to nurture leadership skills in others. They also understand that the world does not revolve around them. As a result, they experience personal satisfaction in whatever they do. Those who know and understand the top tenets of personal and professional leadership consistently come out ahead, while enhancing productivity, profitability, and the bottom line—no matter the circumstances or economic climate.

Layoffs aside, job satisfaction today is at its lowest level in two decades. CEOs are worried about developing new leaders for the future. Middle managers complain of a lack of leadership from above. Motivation and direction appear to have become victims of the economic recession. All of these conditions, however, indicate a much greater problem: an overall lack of real leadership in the workplace and beyond.

Real Leaders Don't Boss is a simple-to-understand, practical resource that helps build leaders in the workplace and in life. This book can help almost anyone grasp what it takes to inspire and lead. With the help of real-life stories and advice from a spectrum of pace-setters, this book will demonstrate how real leaders, with the right direction and guidance, build and empower teams, then quietly stand back and—no matter the economic conditions—observe as others achieve success, which in turn creates the leader's own success.

Put away the textbook definitions with lists of leadership "styles," be they transactional, trans-motivational, or charismatic. *Real Leaders Don't Boss* will show readers aspiring to leadership greatness how to inspire others, how to teach and mentor them, and how to help them achieve their professional and personal goals—while achieving the organization's goals as well.

As a student of real leadership for the past four decades, I believe I know firsthand what it takes to be a real leader. I have studied the philosophies and fundamentals of true leaders across a wide range of businesses and industries, as well as in the public sector. I have been a C-suite executive, military communications specialist (which included a stint in the Office of the Chairman, U.S. Joint Chiefs of Staff), university professor, hospital executive, administrator, consultant, writer, columnist, and entrepreneur. Along the way, I have crossed paths with or worked for a "who's who" of world-class leaders in both the public and private sectors, including Howard S. Holmes and his son Howdy (of the Jiffy Mix company), Charles Walgreen Jr. (of Walgreen's drugstores), Tom Monaghan (founder of

Domino's Pizza), Navy RADM William Thompson (founding president of the U.S. Navy Memorial in Washington, D.C.), U.S. Sen. Richard Lugar, and others. My leadership philosophy has grown and developed into a unique mix of personal perception, vision, historical perspective, diverse workplace experience, and military discipline.

My leadership has been recognized by the U.S. Senate, the U.S. Navy and Army, and many nonprofit and business groups. I have served on five Congressional leadership committees for U.S. Senators and members of the House of Representatives. I have also been privileged to serve on several founding boards of directors and trustees, as well as a number of longstanding boards. Board service enables you to help an organization by utilizing your leadership skills.

Today, I am the California-based founder and president of Eich Associated, a strategic leadership, branding, marketing, communications, and management coaching firm, as well as an adjunct professor at California Lutheran University, a frequent speaker and blogger on leadership and marketing, and a contributor to various business and professional publications.

My academic background includes a doctoral degree in organizational behavior and communication from the University of Michigan, a master's degree in personnel administration from Michigan State University, and a baccalaureate degree in communication from Sacramento State College. I'm also a graduate of Leadership San Francisco and the Stanley K. Lacy's Opportunity Indianapolis leadership program.

In the following pages, I will share the thoughts, observations, and experiences that have helped me recognize what makes a great leader. It's a mold that's built partly on history, partly on experience, and with a big dose of reality. Thus, *Real Leaders Don't Boss* is not another book of quick tips and quips to get employees to do what they are told, a rehash of overused corporate-speak, or essays of worn-out textbook thoughts and ideas from leadership teachers or coaches with little in-the-trenches experience. Instead, this is designed to be an insightful book that delves into the usually overlooked philosophy and fundamentals behind true leadership and how to apply them in life.

In the following pages, I will examine what it takes and how to achieve real leadership. I will draw on my experiences with organizations including the Harter Packing Company, the California Department of Agriculture, the Boy Scouts, Steelcase, Inc., the U.S. Navy and Marine Corps, the University of Michigan, Indiana University Medical Center, Blue Shield of California, and Stanford University Medical Center. I will also help answer the central question, which is not "Where will we find the world's future leaders?" but "How can we develop many more leaders who can chart a long-term course, tackle urgent problems, and teach as they go?"

Joining the U.S. military before I graduated from college was pivotal in helping me learn about the right and wrong ways of leadership. Each of my experiences in the Navy—especially those that involved working with U.S. Marines every day for nearly two years—was a growth opportunity that allowed me to sharpen my leadership skills by observing and interacting with superb leaders. I learned to differentiate between what makes an effective, admirable leader and what does not. Real leadership is definitely not just talking the talk.

In the corporate sector, I have been fortunate to cross paths with many of the best leaders in the world and to observe them in action, especially how they inspire others to greatness—and how the pseudo-leaders don't. My experiences in academia have hopefully helped me hone my mentoring skills so that I can contribute to the discussion about creating a new culture of leaders.

So get ready to improve your work, your life, and the lives of those around you as you learn to understand and embrace the concepts that foster real and true leadership. I welcome your comments at *www.eichassociated.com/contactus.aspx?page=5.*

Chapter 1

The Meaning of Real Leadership

I used to think that running an organization was equivalent to conducting a symphony orchestra. But I don't think that's quite it; it's more like jazz. There's more improvisation.

—Warren Bennis, author of *On Becoming a Leader*

Real leaders are rare in today's fast-moving, financially driven world. In their place are fast-track wannabes and imposters, intent on instant gratification in the form of quick (and unsustainable) bottom-line results. These pseudo-leaders flaunt rigid controls instead of passionate leadership. They seek to drive employees through dominance rather than devotion, and opt for personal glory over the success and interests of others. In part, today's struggling corporate performance, as well as the trend toward dissatisfaction in the workplace, reflect these shortcomings in leadership.

Today's realities, especially with the rocky economic environment and the growing numbers of Millennials (also known as Generation Y, those workers born somewhere between 1980 and 2000) joining the workforce, calls for leadership done right. It demands real leaders who can, and do, make profound differences in the lives of those with whom they interact, who help others achieve greatness in the workplace and in life, and who boost professional and personal bottom lines in the process.

Even strong companies must learn to become more adept at handling marketplace turbulence faster and more skillfully, or their leaders will risk losing their edge, and the company its strength, over the competition. Real leaders recognize that they must maintain the success that has already been accomplished, and the culture, integrity, and brand that defines it. Only then can they continue to institute change successfully and propel a company forward.

Leadership Shortcomings

The leadership gap today is painfully evident. Workers are dissatisfied with their jobs. Middle managers complain of a lack of top-level leadership—one that provides motivation, fosters dedication, promotes recognition, and offers long-term direction. Even corporate leaders recognize the disconnect and its threat to future economic recovery and growth. After all, leaders are needed not only to weather an economic storm, but afterward, to grow and improve battered companies for the future.

Consider some of the facts and figures that, in part, reflect the shortcomings of leadership today:

- ◆ Employee job satisfaction is at an all-time low. It's not a cyclical phenomenon or simply the result of downside economics. The numbers reflect a longtime downward spiral. Only 45 percent of American workers were satisfied in their jobs in 2009, according to a survey released last year by the Conference Board, a group of New York–based global researchers.[1] That's down from 61 percent of workers who were satisfied with their jobs in 1987, the year the survey began.

♦ Talent—more specifically, leadership development—is among the major challenges cited by corporate chiefs today. That's according to "CEO Challenge 2011," a survey of more than 700 CEOs, presidents, and chairmen of companies around the nation by the Conference Board. "CEOs selected the internally focused actions *of improving leadership development/grow talent internally, enhancing the effectiveness of the senior team, providing employee training and development* and *improving leadership succession* as the key strategies to address talent challenges," the Conference Board said in April 2011, when it released its report.[2]

♦ Middle managers aren't happy with their bosses, either, according to an August 2009 report from McKinsey & Company and reported in its *McKinsey Quarterly*. Twenty percent of C-suite and senior executives and 30 percent of middle managers are not at all satisfied with their superiors' performance. That's indicative of "middle managers' overall lack of connection to their current companies," the report said.[3]

♦ Discontent and disconnect brew elsewhere among middle managers. That same McKinsey survey shows:

■ Twenty-seven percent of middle managers say it's risky to their careers to speak up about difficult decisions when their point of view differs from that of more senior managers.

- Only 36 percent of middle managers say they are very likely or extremely likely to remain with their current employer two years from now.

- Huge numbers of top-level executives aren't satisfied with their own performance, especially when it comes to people skills. Only 26 percent of C-suite and senior executives and 17 percent of middle managers are very satisfied with their own overall performance.

No matter who is taking the surveys or keeping track, leadership is lacking. The resulting divide among workers and senior corporate officials has taken on crisis proportions, especially in light of poor economic conditions and the needed presence of leadership vision, guidance, and direction for any recovery.

General Motors, prior to its U.S. government bailout in 2009, was a prime example of leadership failure. The giant automaker was spiraling downward. For decades, its leadership had failed to heed warnings that its labor costs, vehicle quality, and gas-guzzling automobiles would have to change to remain competitive. The company's leadership was unwilling or unable to do something about the high costs of pensions and wages, nor did it improve vehicle quality and fuel efficiency. The buck stopped at the leadership level, and ultimately GM's leadership came up short. They did not react to the demands of the vicissitudes of fortune, and the company ended up on the brink of bankruptcy in 2009 until the U.S. government's controversial $50 billion bailout that stipulated a temporary majority ownership in the company. Whether or not anyone agrees with the bailout, and whatever GM's future, the company is much stronger today because of new leadership that is, at least, trying to connect with reality.

What Is Real Leadership?

A leader is anyone in a decision-making capacity, formal or informal, who advances the strategic goals of the organization, who contributes mightily to institutional performance, and who treats people fairly, honestly, and compassionately. Real leadership goes well beyond that textbook definition, however. Real leaders create the right conditions for others to lead. They do that in part by personifying the Eight Essentials of Effective Leadership:

1. Real leaders don't boss. They are calm in their style, yet have zero tolerance for bullies, who, in any capacity, undermine performance and morale.

2. Real leaders have a central compass. They aspire to do what's right and be a part of something bigger than themselves.

3. Real leaders communicate with clarity, honesty, and directness, and know how to listen.

4. Real leaders have a unique make-up. Their passion translates into a strong corporate culture.

5. Real leaders value and support everyone they lead, out front as well as behind the scenes.

6. Real leaders know when to get out of the way.

7. Real leaders are accessible. They are humble and easily approached.

8. Real leaders know the difference between character and integrity, and why it takes both to succeed.

There are many "leaders" today who manifest some of these traits; a few demonstrate all of them. The great differentiator, though, is that real leaders embrace *all* of these principles *all* of the time. That's a truism whether it involves leaders in business, government, the military, or private life. In the following pages,

I'll talk in-depth about each of these attributes, what they mean, and how you, too, can learn to embrace them. Almost all of us have the potential to lead in some capacity; we simply need to learn how to allow that potential to surface.

◆

President Obama, in a March 2011 speech about the military crisis in Libya, offered an interpretation of leadership in practice: "Leadership is not simply a matter of going it alone and bearing all of the burden ourselves. Real leadership creates the conditions and coalitions for others to step up as well; to work with allies and partners so that they bear their share of the burden and pay their share of the costs; and to see that the principles of justice and human dignity are upheld by all...."[4]

Though he was specifically referring to the U.S. and NATO forces' involvement in Libya, taken out of context and without any partisanship, his ideas build on the general definition of leadership. Real leaders not only take the helm, but they set the stage for others to lead, too.

◆

True and real leadership is a way of life that can and does make the difference in corporate bottom lines (both in good economic times and in bad), in competitive environments, and in the face of external or internal personnel challenges. For proof, look around at those businesses that have remained strong and have even grown during the recent recession. Chances are good that a real and genuine leader who subscribes to the Eight Essentials of Effective Leadership was at the top. Here's a sampling of contemporary leaders across a broad range of industries, each with his or her own unique style, and each a great example of living leadership:

- Vicki Arndt, principal of the California-based Eagleson Arndt Financial Advisors. Arndt is a leader who inspires by her high degree of integrity, incredible personality and sense of humor, knowledge, and her deep sense of service as manifested in the many ways she shows she cares about people. Arndt has led her local Community Leaders Association and Rotary Club and is actively involved in polio eradication. Her leadership style is open, inclusive, and highly motivating.

- David Robinson, retired basketball star, NBA Hall of Famer, and one of the greatest basketball centers of all time. Robinson excelled as a student at the U.S. Naval Academy and led the Midshipmen to three consecutive NCAA basketball tournaments. He was *Sporting News'* College Player of the Year in 1987 and he holds two Olympic gold medals. "The Admiral," as he is known to many, has done plenty off the court, too, especially for inner-city youth. He and his wife, Valerie, founded and provide multi-million-dollar funding to Carver Academy in inner-city San Antonio to help build tomorrow's leaders. Located on property that was occupied by a string of crack houses a decade ago, the school provides an education to mostly low-income children from pre-kindergarten to eighth grade. Carver Academy inspires students to exemplify leadership, discipline, initiative, integrity, service, and faith— the characteristics Robinson embodied at the Naval Academy and throughout his NBA career.

- Pat Riley, a New Yorker, a legendary NBA coach, and the current president of the Miami Heat. Riley has long been recognized for excellence in leadership. The author of *Showtime: Inside the Lakers Breakthrough Season* (Warner Books, 1990), Riley has played with or coached six NBA championship teams. What accounts for Riley's phenomenal success? Though he was an average player during his league career, he became an inspirational coach and a superlative motivator, and is famous for his ability to magically and passionately guide million-dollar players to success.

- ◆ Richard Rush, president of California State University–Channel Islands. As a leader, Rush fosters remarkable optimism among faculty, students, and the community, despite a constant onslaught of budget cuts by the California legislature. Amid tough economic cutbacks, Rush has kept his university nimble while building a firm foundation of academic excellence. He has done so by developing innovative programs that include public-private partnerships. One such partnership is a collaborative nursing degree program with Cottage Hospital in Santa Barbara, California.

- ◆ Susan Murata, currently executive vice president of Silver Star Automotive Group in Southern California. In the middle of a recession, amid the coast-to-coast carcasses of lesser-led car dealerships, Murata exhibits tremendous business acumen and commitment to people and the community. She is an attentive listener and skilled strategist who has a knack for cutting through needless bureaucracy. Other organizations turn to her for enlightened leadership. She has held top leadership positions for her local Chamber of Commerce, Business Roundtable, and many service organizations. Among the secrets to her success are the strength of her personality, her work ethic, and her commitment—not only to volunteerism, but to whatever she finds herself involved in.

◆

Howard S. Holmes was a real leader, both in his community—southeast Michigan—and for his family-owned company, Chelsea Milling Company, which produces the grocery staple Jiffy Mix. In her book, *Jiffy, A Family Tradition*, Cynthia Furlong Reynolds writes, "Howard and Dudley [his twin brother] steered the company through family tragedy, the Depression, World War II, major ups and downs in the economy and the boom-days of the package-mix industry."[5]

Howard Holmes had none of the bluster, egocentric characteristics, or false bravado of some chief executives. Instead, he had an innate comfort in his abilities and shortcomings that enabled employees and colleagues alike to relate to him. His humanity was one of the qualities that distinguished him from being a boss. He never made his employees feel they were inferior or less important. Once he even called me to say he would be a few minutes late to one of our informal breakfast get-togethers. I later discovered the reason why: after a problem in the mill, he had rolled up his sleeves alongside his employees and resolved it. Howard often referred to his employees—his second family—as "knuckleheads," a term they were proud to be called. I don't think the word *boss* was even in his extensive vocabulary.

Nonetheless, times change. His son, Howdy Holmes, faced considerable challenges when he assumed the reins of his family's company, but to his credit, he made changes incrementally and sensitively, reinforcing the core values of Chelsea Milling's culture, teaming openness with interdependence. Under Howdy's leadership as CEO, many suitors have been desirous of purchasing the Jiffy brand, but it is not for sale.

Howdy had to guide Chelsea Milling into the 21st century. That included building new facilities, developing a stronger and larger management team, and establishing an online presence. He did all that while maintaining a tight connection to his employees with the help of what he had learned from his mentors—irreproachable values and personal attention to employees—to which he added calculated risk-taking, management acumen, and strategic thinking.

◆

Logical Though Often Elusive

The logic behind my Eight Essentials of Effective Leadership is deceptively simple. Many of us in business have heard it before: treat people right and do what's right for them, and the business will prosper. The concept seems easy enough. Yet in application, those in leadership roles often fall far short. Most talk about or around the various attributes, but few actually follow through with the understanding, direction, drive, and commitment necessary to be a real leader. True leaders put service above self; empower, don't control; and serve rather than demand to be served. Though making people a priority may not be a popular business model today, it's the only one I can enthusiastically endorse. Throughout my career, I have seen firsthand that the best CEOs subscribe to this approach, and the worst do not.

The Need to Inspire

Real leaders don't dodge opportunities to impact change; they take the challenges head on. Adm. Elmo R. Zumwalt, Jr.

certainly did just that. He led the Navy at a very tumultuous time in the 1970s as then-President Richard Nixon's Chief of Naval Operations. In the Vietnam War era, our country and the military were torn by racism, tension, and turmoil. The Navy faced race riots and sit-down strikes on the docks. Yet Zumwalt saw beyond it all. He was a visionary and a reformer with passion, understanding, resolve, and communications mastery. He transformed operations because he empathized with his young troops' problems—whether they were financial, marital, or caused by long deployments. He was committed to the rights of women and minorities, and knew how to expedite communications and get the job done. And he did it all amid strong opposition from the staid Navy establishment. Nixon appointed Zumwalt over dozens of more senior officers. Many of them had a tough time getting over that. Some never did.

Another real-life leader, this one in the civilian workforce, is Alan Mulally, CEO of Ford Motor Company in Dearborn, Michigan—the same Ford Motor Company that earlier in the last decade was devastated by safety recalls of its popular Explorer SUV. Mulally was named in *Time* magazine's "The World's Most Influential People" in 2009, was a former *Aviation Week* "Person of the Year," and was on the *BusinessWeek* list of "The Best Leaders." Scott Monty, social-media head at Ford, describes his boss Mulally as "the real deal," a leader who inspires by "simply being a human being."[6] Lesser executives would have shunned the incredible challenge to turn Ford Motor Company around, but Mulally took the helm of a company that many corporate experts believed was doing an excellent job of running their business into the ground, inspiring others to believe in its revitalization.

Paul Levy, former CEO of Boston's Beth Israel Deaconess Medical Center, also inspired his employees with his actions. In the medical field, he's a staunch advocate of shared governance—that is, shared decision-making—between physicians and employees. That is not always a popular stance among those in the medical community, especially in the nonprofit sector. Yet amid the economic meltdown of 2009, Levy took cuts to his salary and benefits package, and boldly encouraged hospital employees to do the same in order to save the jobs of the hospital's lower-wage earners.

Real-life leaders such as Zumwalt, Mulally, and Levy embrace effective leadership, the nature of which inspires others. Many others in positions of power and control do not. The result, as the McKinsey survey reflects, is that workers are disconnected and disenfranchised from their companies.

◆

Leadership—formal and informal—exists at all levels of every organization. In the 1990s, as California Lutheran University's vice president of marketing and communications, I worked with five exceptional leaders. None had big titles, big offices, big salaries, or big staffs. They didn't seek power, the limelight, or credit. Yet their words and deeds personified the Eight Essentials of Effective Leadership, and they created a culture of leadership around them. They were always there in a pinch, were never too busy to help others, and always went the extra mile to provide superior results:

- ◆ Dennis Bryant of Conferences and Events. He was the motor who kept the independent educational establishment functioning, the "Ernie Pyle" of the collegiate troops.
- ◆ Della Greenlee of the Foundations office. A gifted writer and story-teller, she was the master at establishing enduring relationships with the foundation world.

- Jose "Joe" Morales of Printing Services. A superb teacher and role model, he could write the book on quality customer service.

- Vanessa Webster-Smith of Auxiliary Services. A staunch champion and mentor to those students who work for her, she was delightful and always ready to help.

- Katie Binz Sims of University Relations. Highly ethical, moral, and selfless, with a tremendous depth of commitment, she had an inspiring effect on everyone and an uncanny ability to attract others from all across the campus to assist in branding the organization.

All five of these university leaders embodied what Robert Greenleaf meant by the term *servant leadership*. They displayed empathy, mentored student and colleague alike, honored the faith institution's past by respecting those who preceded them, and continuously strived for the common good.

◆

Health Hazards

Beyond bottom lines, poor or non-existent leadership can be hazardous to employees' health. A Swedish study involving researchers from Stockholm University and Karolinska Institute, as well as University College London and the Finnish Institute of Occupational Health, found that a bad boss can create unnecessary and debilitating stress among employees. The group followed the heart health of more than 3,100 male employees, aged 19 to 70, in Stockholm, Sweden, between 1992 and 2003. Workers who rated their bosses least competent had a 25-percent-higher risk of serious heart disease, whereas those who rated their bosses as most effective had the lowest risk.

"This study is the first to provide evidence of a prospective, dose-response relationship between concrete managerial behaviors and objectively assessed heart disease among employees," Anna Nyberg, coauthor of the study, said when the study was released in 2009. "Enhancing managers' skills—regarding providing employees with information, support, power in relation to responsibilities, clarity in expectations, and feedback—could have important stress-reducing effects on employees and enhance the health at workplaces," added Nyberg. Study participants were asked to rate the leadership styles of their senior managers in terms of how clearly they set out goals for employees and to assess how good a manager was in terms of communicating and providing feedback. Study results showed that those who created the most stress had a lack of empathy and an inability to delegate, as well as a refusal to listen to staff.[7]

Leadership Learned

Great leaders can be born into a culture of leaders—the Kennedys, for example—but birthright is no guarantee that someone will become the real deal. Real leaders are made; they learn through trial and error, and are nurtured and developed through time. Too often we hear things such as "he (or she) is a natural-born leader." A person may, indeed, have the make-up, temperament, patience, and vision to lead, but without the right attitude, experience, approach, and training, that individual's "knack" for leadership doesn't translate into real leadership.

Whether leaders are made or born is "an old question that has dogged academicians and practitioners alike for centuries," says Michael Bradbury, former Ventura County district attorney and prosecutor, teacher, and leader. Bradbury also said:

The answer is they are born and also made. We have all heard the stories of natural leaders who, after an undistinguished career, emerge a hero in combat environments by leading their men out of danger or to take an objective. They instill confidence and courage in others who then find the strength to continue to fight and help others. Winston Churchill, I believe, fell into this category. He was pilloried at times for his perceived lack of leadership but as prime minister rallied the people and saved England during World War II. He was then promptly thrown out of office. But, I believe that more leaders are made than born. There are leadership academies everywhere. Most prep schools advertise that they develop future leaders. Our colleges and universities pick up this mantra and it dominates their marketing material. And, of course, the military promises, in its multimillion-dollar recruitment efforts, to build tomorrow's leaders.[8]

Most real leaders aren't born with some innate ability transforming them into magnets that attract others to follow them. They may have expectations placed on them to rise above their present situation or environment; they may even have an inborn strong desire to serve others and to accomplish something unique. In most cases, however, leadership skills are developed and honed in the battlefield of life, where leaders discover their drive, passion, and wisdom. Through trial and error, winning and losing, a leader's self-confidence grows, aplomb develops, and risk-taking becomes a more accepted path. Observation of other leaders in action and service to others often becomes very important.

Honing those leadership skills can happen outside the workplace, too. One of the many leadership "laboratories" helpful to me was my college fraternity, Sigma Phi Epsilon. Serving my fraternity brothers in different roles afforded numerous types of leadership training. I learned quickly how to deal with adversity and constructive criticism, as well as how to improve, grow, and handle increased responsibility. Perhaps most important, the significance of serving others was reinforced time and again, as was the value of a close-knit and open-minded community.

Being chosen by my peers to be captain of a varsity sports team was also an important learning experience for me. As captains are normally chosen to help inspire and energize a team, I saw this opportunity as a test of my leadership skills. I realized I had to not only step up my performance as an athlete but also to set an example by the way I practiced, helped younger players, and reinforced the coaches' goals for the season. My coaches instilled in me the belief that effective captains helped develop and teach the less experienced among us just as business leaders strengthen their employees' skills. Whether you are a captain of a sports team, an academic decathlon, a debate team, or a work team, you learn to be a better leader by practical experience.

Round-the-Clock Leadership

Amway co-founder and NBA Orlando Magic owner Rich DeVos, whom I got to know while I was senior vice president of a large Midwestern hospital, knew what he was talking about when he wrote in his book *Ten Powerful Phrases for Positive People* (Center Street, 2008), "Leadership is what you do at home." Again, it's about living the ideals in your private, professional, and social life; passing them on; and motivating those around you.

◆

"If your actions inspire others to dream more, learn more, do more and become more, you are a leader."

—John Quincy Adams[9]

◆

Howard Holmes, mentioned previously, did just that. Before his death in 2001, Holmes, as CEO of Chelsea Milling, was a trailblazer in the packaged-foods industry. Along the way, he always had time to listen and share his knowledge with others. Today, a plaque hangs on the wall of the mill that reads:

"Howard Sumner Holmes' devotion to the noblest principles of living and his unfailing generosity with his time were qualities for which he will long be remembered with great affection." Holmes' real-life leadership rubbed off on his son, Howdy, who succeeded his father as president and CEO of Chelsea Milling in the mid-1990s. With his father's same inspiring approach, Howdy was able to make the necessary adjustments to shepherd the 105-year-old company through today's turbulent business times and strongly position it for the future.

Howdy Holmes demonstrated his considerable sense of leadership skill long before rejoining the family business. A racecar driver by training, he was named "Rookie of the Year" at the Indianapolis 500 in 1979. Off the track, he proved to be an inspiring leader for young fans, too. I once watched him work his magic with a group of Cub Scouts in Ann Arbor, Michigan.

It was an evening I shall never forget. Within a few minutes, Howdy Holmes had captivated the group, and they began sliding on their haunches across the gym floor to get closer to him. As he spoke about physical fitness, clean living, pursuing dreams, and the importance of not making mistakes that could forever destroy aspirations, I knew right then that this young man would become a truly inspiring leader. Howdy spoke with the children—not at them—and was well-organized, humorous, and clearly passionate about his message.

Leadership Today

Today's workplace is a far cry from the insular corporate environment of workplaces of the past. The marketplace is global, wired, and constantly changing. These facts cannot be excuses for poor leadership. These are simply the realities that necessitate different approaches and shifts in leadership. Though the values of true leadership are timeless, the application must change as business does. Let's look more closely at the old and the new approaches to leadership:[10]

Yesterday	Today
Simply manage those around you.	Teach and lead by example.
Lead by fear, intimidation, and threats.	Lead by teaching, empowering, and mentoring.
"My way or the highway."	Define the parameters and then allow workers to innovate.
Relatively predictable external environment that complemented simplistic, more stratified work environment.	Team approach to solving problems.
Local, regional, or national market.	Global external environment; very fast to market.
Stable markets with well-defined niches.	Marketplace more volatile, more ambiguous, more competitive, and more risk is associated with decisions made.
Leaders recruited from outside the organization.	Companies develop many of their leaders from within with the help of leadership pipelines that train, educate, and develop candidates from practically every level within the company.
Autocratic leaders, with CEO usually making the decision himself or with one or two others in decision-making capacity.	Real leaders more humble, use executive teams in decision-making.
Leaders and boards of directors primarily white males.	Boardrooms more diverse; women lead major companies, though many argue the glass ceiling remains.

"That doesn't, however, mean the qualities that always have distinguished true leaders don't still hold true," says attorney Bradbury. "Those qualities include honesty, leading by example, demonstrating character in all that one does, not asking someone to do what you would not, being kind and understanding, and being decisive and fair," adds Bradbury, who also excels at grooming talented young attorneys for careers in judicial and legislative branches of government, and who is the first district attorney to be elected twice as president of the California District Attorneys Association. He continues:

> Leaders today must understand that they can no longer simply rely on "gut feelings" and doing it the way it was always done. The new leaders must be inquisitive and genuinely interested in change and learning. For example, they should become familiar with the new and rapidly expanding social media. A leader should learn from his/her employees and seek out opportunities to do so.... Older leaders must return to [leadership] "school" and learn to meld the new thinking, global and otherwise, with the tried-and-true characteristics of great leaders.[11]

Unfortunately, not all the developments and changes in today's workplace are for the better. The trend toward excess in top-level management compensation and benefits has created significant challenges in the sphere of leadership, especially when considering changing demographics and attitudes in the workplace.

The younger workforce—including growing numbers of Millennials—is far less enamored of traditional organizations, according to author Ron Alsop.[12] These workers tend to be more independent and less likely to remain in the same job for as long as their counterparts of the past. That creates major challenges for today's managers. Again, these are not insurmountable challenges, and they come with big rewards. But it takes new stimuli and incentives to retain these technologically savvy, bright, and environmentally conscious young minds, including more interesting assignments, frequent performance feedback, and company-supported affinity groups.

Adding to the challenge, as the gulf in salaries and benefits between the top and bottom ranks of many organizations exceeds acceptable bounds, workers are much less likely to feel compelled to work harder, have a sense of loyalty, or feel responsible to help solve a company's pressing challenges. These undervalued employees instead point to the C-suite with its bloated salaries, perks, and bonuses, and say, "Let them solve it!" Factor in today's rocky economic environment that has forced many companies to eliminate some of their workforce in order to survive, and the fact that the traditional expectation that those remaining will pick up the slack doesn't necessarily hold true anymore.

The General Motors bailout and takeover is a prime example of the chasm between boardrooms, line employees, and market realities. Another example is the insurance giant American International Group (AIG), which the federal government bailed out to the tune of $85 billion and a majority ownership in 2008. In the case of both companies, the leadership enjoyed exorbitant salaries and lavish perks as the markets crumbled around them. (As of July 2011, AIG continued to struggle as it appears GM continued to rebuild.)

The challenges of the 21st century aren't insurmountable. They are simply new and different, and require real, enlightened leadership to step up and take the helm. Some companies and leaders already are doing just that, according to the Hay Group's sixth annual *Best Companies for Leadership Study* and *Top 20* released in January 2011. The 2010 survey involved more than 1,825 organizations worldwide. Among the approaches top companies have adopted to improve their efficiency and competitive positioning are diversifying their workforces and moving away from hierarchical—top-down—leadership, the study reports.[13]

Economic Challenges

Keeping a company and its staff afloat in tough economic times requires special leadership. To maintain the forward momentum is an even greater challenge, even for real leaders.

Harold S. Edwards, president and CEO of California-based Limoneira Company, a major global producer of citrus, is one of those leaders focused on maintaining his company's strategic and community edge despite today's bumpy economy, and he's quick to admit it is not easy:

> Strategically plotting Limoneira's course through an extremely treacherous economic downturn has tested me. Keeping the board focused on strategic and governance issues and the management team focused on managerial issues during the recent unprecedented downturn in the U.S. economy has been the most challenging situation for me since assuming the helm at Limoneira. Plotting our strategic course while managing significant real estate exposure has been a true test for me.
>
> Being able to display the courage and confidence in specific ventures while making the difficult decisions to exit others (sometimes at a loss) while moving the hearts and minds of Limoneira's board, its managers, and its shareholders forward toward greater shareholder value has been the challenge. Diversification has allowed us to weather the storm. Limoneira is in position to create significant value as the local and regional economies heal. Keeping everyone on the board and within management rowing in the same direction

and focused on solving problems (as opposed to only identifying them) has allowed us to sail through this difficult phase intact. Keeping Limoneira's hearts and minds together has been a true challenge for me and one of my greatest professional tests to date.[14]

Through all of these challenges, Edwards has remained a leader who demonstrates a tremendous confidence, positive image, and a real gift for building consensus among different groups involved in his operation. These, as well as the other qualities he mentioned, have helped his company weather the storm.

All types of leaders are tested by the economic realities of today. Some survive—and even thrive—while others do not. As Edwards's words attest, it can be rough even for companies with strong leadership. It is easy to succeed—or at least wear the trappings of success in terms of profits—when everyone is buying and marketplaces are thriving. It is far more difficult when markets are stagnant, but that is when real leaders rise to the occasion, rally their troops and their communities, and make a difference.

Understanding Real Leadership

Perhaps one of the simplest ways to better understand the power of real leadership is to consider what you like and what you don't like in a leader. Consider some of the following questions as they relate to those in leadership roles. There are no right or wrong answers to these questions. Instead, your answers should help you put together a list of favorable and unfavorable traits in a leader:

- ◆ What do you admire about your leader or leaders in general?

- ◆ How do you react to particular approaches this leader takes?

- Does your leader foster effective relationships with you and others?

- Does your leader encourage you to stretch, and does she or he empower you to further develop your skill set?

- What makes you want to do just the opposite of what a person in a leadership role says?

- How do you react when someone orders you to do something rather than suggest an approach that might work, or help you come up with the answer?

Now ask yourself, "What is it I truly dislike about the trait and why?" Is it because of the attitude it conveys, the approach that the leader takes, or simply the content of the message? Figuring out the specific strengths and weaknesses of the leaders you know can help you in your own quest for real leadership. Keep in mind that if you model a certain behavior, others likely will follow your lead. Are your actions commensurate with your goals and ideals?

You Can Do It, Too

Consider one of the 20th century's greatest leaders, President Franklin Delano Roosevelt, who led our country through one of its most difficult times despite his own personal ill health. FDR was a true servant leader who put the well-being of the country and its people—his "company" and its "employees"—well ahead of his own. Roosevelt was elected president at the height of the Great Depression, and was able to inspire and guide the country through most of World War II. Roosevelt personally was wealthy, yet he was a master motivator of the masses who could inspire others by placing their well-being above his own, providing clear direction and goals, giving his team—the administration as well as the American people—the tools they needed to accomplish those goals, and then offering encouragement and moral support all along the way.

To develop your own servant leadership potential, practice the art of sacrifice for others rather than thinking of having subordinates or followers. Champion your team, troops, or staff by always helping and promoting them. Set the most enviable example and let your actions demonstrate what serving others truly means. Take FDR's lead: put the greater good of the organization above your own, set clear direction and goals for your organization and its people, never ask more of others than you do of yourself, and provide encouragement and praise along the way.

Takeaway

- ◆ Real leaders make profound differences in the lives of those around them, they help others achieve greatness in the workplace and in life spaces, and they boost professional and personal bottom lines in the process.

- ◆ Today's leadership gap is very real. Employee satisfaction with its leaders is at an all-time low, middle managers aren't satisfied with their bosses, and leaders admit their own behavior often is lacking.

- ◆ Real leadership is a 24/7 occupation and lifestyle.

- ◆ Real leaders do not seek the limelight. Rather, they embody the true qualities of effective leadership; they are always available, are never too busy to help others, and always go the extra mile.

- ◆ Poor leadership leads not only to unhealthy bottom lines, but to unhealthy employees, too.

- ◆ Leadership is not a birthright. Real leaders are nurtured and developed.

- Real leadership shouldn't be only at the top of an organization; it must pervade all levels.

- Today's workspace and marketplace are wired, global, and changing. That means leaders must change, too, or companies risk losing their competitive edge.

- Real leadership is not about amassing personal power; it's about the ability to unleash the strengths of others and in turn create a culture of success.

Chapter 2

Real Leaders Don't Boss

My definition of leadership is the combination of vision and selfless consensus building.

—Harold Edwards, president and CEO,
Limoneira Company

osses certainly are not in short supply; real leaders are the elusive commodity. In the workplace and throughout life, each of us encounters leadership behaviors or organizational policies that we like or admire, and that we may try to adapt to our own business situations and lives. Conversely, we all know of, have seen, or have suffered firsthand from those bosses with not-so-admirable behaviors and policies that often are ineffective, counterproductive, and sometimes offensive. Of those people and their behaviors and policies we think, "Absolutely no way will I ever act that way!"

Follow-through on that statement, however, may be another matter. We are usually taught to boss, not to lead, and in many cases, bosses are the most prevalent role models. Rare today is the individual who inspires others with focus, trust, strategic know-how, and an instinct for knowing what's important, along with the ability to selflessly rally and mobilize his or her troops.

Leader Versus Boss

Unfortunately, many self-professed and corporate-appointed "leaders" are little more than bosses. Some have a few hours of instant leadership training. Others claim they are in the position because of their "natural knack" for the job, and still others simply find themselves saddled with the responsibilities. Sadly, any brief or extended training aside, the end result is still a boss and not a real leader.

Throughout my four-decade-long career in a variety of sectors reporting to all types of decision-makers, I have seen all kinds of chief executives—good and bad—in action. I also have dealt with a few bosses who were philanderers, racists, bullies, and egomaniacs with anger-management problems. Many were intellectually bright, but their behaviors undermined the success their organizations could have achieved with real leadership. For example, one philanderer had an executive assistant who he insisted be promoted despite her incompetence. It turns out she had filed a sexual discrimination suit against him. Another executive took office parties as a license to dance cheek-to-cheek with employees. It seems he also had a reputation of playing around after hours with his staffers.

Consider how the approach and behavior of a real leader differs from that of a boss when it comes to a few key workplace issues:

- ◆ **Corporate success:** A *leader* focuses on long-term results and positions his or her company for ongoing success. A *boss* is too concerned about the next quarter's bottom line to have a big-picture perspective.

- **Employees:** A *leader* is a champion for his or her employees. A *boss* sees employees as a means to an end.

- **Communication:** A *leader* connects directly with the board, shareholders, customers, suppliers, *and* with the employee base, and takes the time to listen and respond in a thoughtful and humble manner that values all these people. A *boss* pays lip service to employees but is more focused on his or her own well-being.

- **Respect for others:** A *leader* shows congeniality and respect to everyone regardless of rank. A *boss* is pleasant and charming to executives, while indifferent or demeaning toward those he or she supervises.

- **Conflict resolution:** A *leader* recognizes that conflict is inevitable at one time or another. He or she deals with it by channeling it to constructive ends. A *boss* often creates conflict but fails to deal with it effectively.

- **Behavior of managers:** A *leader* prohibits demeaning, disrespectful, or verbally abusive behavior from his or her managers. A *boss* ignores that kind of behavior and may exhibit it himself or herself.

- **Respecting the personal life of an employee:** A *leader* recognizes that employees enjoy a private and personal life outside of the business and appreciates the need to maintain a work/life balance for well-being and productivity. A *boss* overloads his team with many tasks and impossible due dates, then micromanages them.

- **Getting the job done:** A *leader* works to remove obstacles for his or her employees, provides the necessary resources, and expedites processes to make it easier for others to accomplish their jobs. A *boss* creates roadblocks that get in the way of the job, lead to pointless extra work, and create unnecessary frustration.

The Ugly Executive

The Ugly American by William J. Lederer and Eugene Burdick (W.W. Norton, 1999), originally published in 1958, was required high school reading when I was in school. It describes a character who has little sensitivity toward or interest in others. Little did I realize at the time that later in the workplace I would meet head-on the ugly American's cousin, the "ugly executive." A leader's primary responsibility is to articulate a vision and establish a set of strategies that unleashes the creativity, freedom, and individual potential of the workforce. The behavior of the "ugly executive" drains an organization of critically needed energy, strength, creativity, passion, and loyalty, and threatens essential relationships with key constituencies.

Unattractive Behaviors

Who are these ugly executives we all have likely encountered at one time or another? In many cases their egomaniacal actions drag their companies down with them. Here are a few of the most offensive traits and the behaviors associated with the ugly executive:

- ◆ **Lying.** An organization's CEO tells one of his managers that her employment contract for the new fiscal year is somewhere on his desk, but he isn't exactly sure where it is specifically. Time passes and no contract materializes, so the manager asks again about her contract. This time, the CEO snaps at her,

"Well, you're getting paid, aren't you?" The manager asks the HR department chief about the contract, and she honestly tells the manager that the president has not requested they draft a contract for her.

- **Egotism.** The leader of the C-suite directs her executive assistant to call the hotel where she plans to stay on an upcoming business trip and to secure the largest or most impressive suite of rooms. If it is not up to her standards in size or opulence, she will demand another hotel.

- **Arrogance.** Several company employees are on a commercial flight or company plane, and the executive among them sits apart from the others and ignores them for the duration of the flight.

- **Tyranny.** At the last minute, the boss decides to have lunch in his office and commands an administrative assistant to go outside the building to get his meal. After he is finished eating, he chastises the assistant for the "poor quality" of the meal as he shoves the food tray away in a demeaning manner.

- **Romantic liaison.** One CEO wanted to hire a young woman he was sleeping with (he was married at the time). Her credentials didn't match the criteria for any vacant jobs at the company, so he created a new executive position by combining elements from the duties of other vice presidents. The young woman was unable to do the work, so the vice presidents got their assignments back. But the woman remained on the payroll as "an executive without portfolio."

- **Racism and/or sexism.** The company chairman periodically invites his vice presidents, all of whom are white males, to his favorite restaurant for lunch, and proceeds to rattle off a string of racist and/or sexist jokes. The company's ethnic make-up—as well as that of the managers—reflects the CEO's biased attitudes, too.

Bullies on the Job

As a teen during summers spent working at manual labor in the peach orchards throughout Yuba and Sutter counties in California, I watched how hard others worked alongside me, and that reinforced the importance of a strong work ethic. One or two situations also taught me that bullies have no place in any workplace. However, that does not mean they do not exist.

As a young adult, I worked as a fruit inspector for the California Department of Agriculture, checking the quality of the products farmers would bring to be inspected before being sold to the canneries. It was up to me—from all appearances a young kid—to reject rotten products or those of unacceptable quality. One day after I had rejected a particularly rotten truckload of peaches, a clearly irate—and intoxicated—rancher stormed up to me, obviously intent on bullying me into submission. He ripped his shirt off; the buttons flew into the air as he raised his fists to fight. Instead of fighting, though, I attempted to reason with him. Eventually I told him that if he did not want to accept my ruling on his load of fruit—which likely represented an important portion of his income—I would be happy to call in the district supervisor for a second opinion. I did, and my supervisor rejected the fruit even more resoundingly than I had. The dejected farmer backed down, drove off, and probably dumped his fruit that no doubt he knew was unacceptable.

In addition to being rather startled by the encounter, I recognized that I had done the right thing—to reason rather than to fight verbally or physically, and to remain true to my ideals and directions.

More on Sexist Behavior

Too many times I've watched highly capable women passed over for promotions or marginalized, not because of their lack of ability, but simply because they are women. Here are several examples (the names and companies are withheld to protect the individuals):

- An African-American woman held a variety of positions in the organization, all of which stymied her abilities. It almost seemed as if the firm didn't know—or care—what to do with her. She was well-versed in the region and knew most of the CEOs in the city personally—few could match that asset alone—which enabled her to open doors. She was street smart, had class, and was very resilient. I eventually realized that the insecure CEO had marginalized her because he considered her a threat and was uncomfortable in her presence.

- An older woman had devoted most of her working life to her employer. She had a superb grasp of the history, values, and traditions of the business and community, and was the go-to person for a variety of information. Many of the males on staff—including the CEO—rather than recognize her strengths, saw her as "over the hill" and a busy-body who was too old to be of value.

- A younger woman at another organization was incredibly industrious, was refined, and had an infectious sense of humor. She did her job well, and her peers knew they always could count on her. But her supervisor rarely supported her, even when he knew it was the right thing to do. He was one of those particularly insecure bosses who smiled up the organization, sucking up to his superiors, and frowned down it, disrespecting or ignoring those in lesser positions.

+ Another woman at a different organization was the perfect employee. She had a sense of humor, was highly skilled in her job, and knew the right people in business and leadership roles throughout the region. Yet she remained in the same job and was always passed over for the prime assignments. Instead of capitalizing on the woman's strengths, the chief executive considered her a nuisance.

Racism Intolerable

One of the biggest workplace detriments regarding racism, as with many of the other unacceptable workplace behaviors mentioned here, is that its opposite—diversity—yields powerful advantages. A few of these include:

+ **Innovation, curiosity, and creativity.** Leaders are receptive to how ideas are created, and understand that without new ideas, they will lose a significant competitive edge. Bold, new ideas seldom take place in a vacuum; they happen at intersections and often are the result of a spark generated by the intermingling of people with different perspectives, life circumstances, and cultures.

+ **Customer value and brand loyalty.** Whether a business has domestic or international customers, a diverse employee base in marketing, sales, product design, and other aspects is important because we live and work in an increasingly global society. Companies need to acknowledge this, or risk losing credibility and customers who do not want to deal with companies projecting outdated ideologies.

- **Talent pool**. Recruiting employees from emerging markets makes undeniably sound business sense. Boards of directors, senior management, middle management, and front-line employees must be diverse in order to attract this emerging talent. Otherwise, the emerging workforce will go elsewhere.

Sets of Standards

In an attempt to deal with the ugly executive, some boardrooms adopt certain behavioral expectations for top management. Even so, the ugly executive isn't always held accountable. That doesn't mean, however, that you or your fellow employees should lower your own standards of conduct.

Fortunately, some companies do look at diversity and solutions to other significant issues as essential attributes for success in the global marketplace. "The best leaders are learning they must check their egos at the door and become increasingly sensitive to diversity, generational and geographical issues," says Rick Lash, director in Hay Group's Leadership and Talent Practice and co-leader of Hay Group's *Best Companies for Leadership*.[1] According to Hay Group's January 2011 study, among the Top 20 companies for leadership:

- 90 percent actively recruit cultural minorities.
- 95 percent say cultural diversity has helped their organization become more effective.
- 100 percent actively manage a pool of successors for mission-critical roles.
- 100 percent have a sufficient number of qualified internal candidates who are ready to assume

open leadership positions at all levels of the organization.

◆ 58 percent have a high proportion of women in senior leadership.

◆ 95 percent say helping employees achieve a work-life balance is a priority.

Unacceptable Behavior

What is your company's policy, if any, toward ugly executives? If you're not sure of the answer, chances are your company turns the other cheek. Can you figure out why? Most likely, the company is unable or unwilling to take the necessary stand of zero tolerance toward these behaviors, which are unprofessional, counter-productive, and absolutely, positively don't belong in the workplace.

Is there anything you can do to negate or marginalize the negativity from these employees? Practice zero tolerance. If this person is a boss, confront senior management on the issue. Or, if management continues to tolerate the behavior, pack your briefcase and move on.

Leaders Make the Difference

The real leader is the antithesis of the ugly executive, and his or her influence can and does make a positive difference in business and industry, whether an organization is corporate, private, governmental, or some other entity. Leaders connect with those around them and spur actions. It's not a unique concept, but it is an essential one for leadership and long-term success.

One of the most effective leaders in recent memory is Robert Gates, former U.S. Secretary of Defense in both the George W. Bush and Obama administrations. A big part of Gates's effectiveness is his superb ability to form close, professional relationships and partnerships with those around him. As Defense Secretary, Gates had a close working relationship with the President of the United States. Gates understood President Obama's needs and met them time after time. As a real leader, Gates understands the importance of building solid relationships, and that establishing and nurturing alliances with others expedites the accomplishment of goals. Perhaps Gates gained that essential insight from his years as a university president at Texas A&M—a role that requires a leader to satisfy many different constituencies.

The Zumwalt Difference

When President Richard Nixon appointed Admiral Elmo R. "Bud" Zumwalt Chief of Naval Operations in 1970, the nation was embroiled in the Vietnam War. Reenlistment rates had plummeted as youth rejected the military in general, and the Navy, which had largely ignored racial integration, was forced to deal with well-publicized racial incidents aboard ships as well as dockside strikes. In other words, the Navy was mired in discontent, much of it caused by a huge disconnect between bosses (management) and staff (officers and enlisted personnel). Real leadership was lacking. Nixon knew this and recognized that rocky times called for a leader, not a boss or a bully. Zumwalt was a leader who genuinely cared about others and his organization, the U.S. Navy.

Zumwalt, who had served as Commander of Naval Forces and Chief of the Naval Advisory Group for Vietnam, was appointed over 33 senior officers. At age 49, he was the youngest officer to hold the nation's top Navy post and the position of admiral.[2] He was a go-getter, a visionary, and a communicator, and he knew how to listen.

His four-year tour as Chief of Naval Operations was characterized by his herculean efforts to foster dignity, respect, service, and honor among all naval personnel by meeting with them, listening to their suggestions for improvement, empowering them, and ensuring that their needs were better met by their commanders. At the same time, he never forgot the primary mission: to enhance the Navy's ability as a superior fighting force. The policy directives Zumwalt issued during his tenure were called "Z-grams," and many remained standard operating procedure after he left his post.[3]

After Zumwalt's death in January 2000, he was honored in the U.S. Congressional Record in a statement by Sen. Russell Feingold:

> As CNO (Chief Naval Officer), Adm. Zumwalt tackled some of the most divisive and challenging issues not just to hit the Navy, but society at large. And we're still trying to conquer some of them. Adm. Zumwalt crusaded for a fair and equal Navy. He fought to promote equality for minorities and women at a time of considerable racial strife in our country and at a time of deeply entrenched institutional racism and sexism in the Navy. He pushed so hard against the establishment that he almost lost his job. But Zumwalt prevailed and instituted a host of personnel reforms....[4]

A great leader on and off the battlefield, Zumwalt was eulogized by President Bill Clinton at his funeral at the U.S. Naval Academy Chapel in Annapolis:

> As much as any other leader in our entire history, Americans could always count on Bud Zumwalt to do the right thing. The midshipmen here learn a lot about honor, commitment, and courage. All his life, he exemplified those virtues. His bravery in World War II, in Korea, what he did in Vietnam, his physical courage

and leadership led him to become the youngest Chief of Naval Operations in our history. But beyond his physical courage, Bud Zumwalt stood out for his moral courage and for saying what he thought was right, regardless of the consequences....[5]

The Edwards Transformation

We also find these leaders outside of the military branches. Limoneira's Harold Edwards is another transformational leader who cares about employees and the community and who can handle whatever he encounters. He defines leadership as "...the combination of vision and selfless consensus building."[6]

Founded in 1893, Limoneira had been a pioneer in California agriculture. When Edwards took over the leadership of Limoneira, the company was treading water, relying on its past achievements instead of looking to the future. Edwards was a visionary who could see potential and, like Adm. Zumwalt, he knew how to build toward the future. As a leader, he also knew how to build consensus. Instead of coming in with big plans—his plans—to change everything, Edwards worked long and hard to forge community and corporate partnerships and encourage the concept of "stewardship" of resources, part of the foundation that once had made the company great. Limoneira was transformed. Today it is the largest producer of avocados and lemons in the United States, and oversees more than 7,000 acres in production. The company is also a major force in real estate in the Southern California region. [7]

Public annual shareholder meetings can be raucous affairs, where it is often difficult for a company's leader to handle irate shareholders, let alone satisfy them, while still maintaining a friendly and professional manner. But the latter is no problem for Edwards, a master communicator and listener who manages it all with ease. He discusses corporate concepts and strategies for the future and patiently answers shareholder inquiries. He is deliberate, careful in explaining the company's decisions, and unruffled, no matter how demanding the questions or the temperament of shareholders. He handles difficult situations with the utmost diplomatic skill, and never bullies or puts down a shareholder, no matter the question.

I've watched Harold Edwards in action many times, but perhaps the most telling was at a recent Limoneira annual meeting. During the question and answer period, he took all the shareholder questions, and patiently and thoughtfully answered each one, so no one felt snubbed even when the questions were disquieting or impertinent. He then offered to meet with each questioner privately if he hadn't answered their question to their complete satisfaction. Edwards's desire to go above and beyond to better inform his shareholders is testament to his desire "to teach and to develop" one of the company's most important constituencies, a signature leadership quality. It has also enabled him to transform his business model by gaining consensus among an ever-diverse set of stakeholders.

The agricultural business Edwards manages has been passed down from generation to generation since California was settled. Throughout time, the large ranches and parcels of land have been divided among an increasing pyramid of heirs. Left alone, this process has resulted in small pockets being developed independently, often resulting in a loss of contiguous land for agriculture. By working with individual families and their heirs, Harold has been able to transform family lands into a collaborative corporate entity where heirs can pass down stock without loss of agricultural lands.

The Fleming Factor

Yet another great change-maker and principled leader who cared about those around him was Robben W. Fleming.

Before his death in 2010 at age 93, he served in various leadership posts, including president of the University of Michigan, chancellor of the University of Wisconsin, and president of the Corporation for Public Broadcasting. A professor of law and an arbitrator, he also held labor and industrial relations posts at the universities of Wisconsin and Illinois.

Fleming was a courageous spokesperson for racial justice, an ardent critic of the Vietnam War, and a staunch advocate for nonviolence. In the tumultuous 1960s, as buildings at colleges and universities across the nation were being torched by student protesters, Fleming always listened and truly cared about the staff, students, and community around him. During one violent student protest when he was chancellor at Wisconsin, he reportedly called the police to arrest the protesters (which they did, hauling them off to jail), and then personally bailed them out of jail using his own money. At the University of Michigan later during similarly unsteady times, Fleming used his labor negotiation skills, patience, and humor to help the university weather that era, avoiding the destructive confrontations that affected many other universities.

◆

For me, the Navy was a tale of working with some of the best and most effective leaders, as well as some of those not-so-stellar bosses.

My first duty assignment was the brig, specifically the Correctional Center at Naval Base, Great Lakes, Illinois. Officially, that meant I was a correctional counselor in a prison run by Marines. I was assigned to Senior Chief Personnelman Harry Johnson, who was responsible for my orientation, supervision, and development. Johnson truly was a real leader. He knew the business and was experienced onshore and at sea. He was intelligent, professional, and wise. His leadership style was to do the right thing at the right time and in accordance with Navy regulations. He also taught me the importance of being punctual, completing my assignments on time or early, and the value of discipline accompanied by fairness. He set the right example at all times and led in this manner.

Senior Chief Johnson was a highly capable manager with an abundance of "white-knuckle" experience solving problems under pressure with limited resources while underway at sea throughout his 25-plus years in the Navy. He attended to his duties in the brig with discipline, precision, and care. Like many seasoned sailors, he carried himself with a gruff exterior, an active mind, and a well-concealed soft heart. I remember late one evening, several prisoners escaped from the brig. Marines—some barely clad and armed with loaded rifles—were dispatched from their barracks to cordon off the brig, while others were dispatched in hot pursuit of the escapees. It so happened that at the same time this was going on, my wife, Joan, arrived at the brig to pick me up. Johnson sent two Marines to escort her to safety inside our offices. Their idea of "safety" was to place Joan in the "bullpen," an area where peaceful prisoners were held under observation. When Johnson found out, he promptly moved her, remarking, "Well, Joan, now that you've been properly oriented to a military correctional facility, do you want to enlist?" His wit defused an otherwise-tense situation, probably saved my marriage, and endeared my wife to him forever.

Bosses are often more concerned about how they look in such a situation, but Johnson's decisiveness and humor were singularly focused on the well-being of others and what his judgment told him needed to be done.

◆

Bosses Versus Leaders and the Millennials

We have all encountered the boss who takes the one-size-fits-all approach. That kind of disconnect and resulting disenfranchisement of employees happens all the time in today's multi-cultural, multi-racial, and multi-age workplace. That is, in part, why worker satisfaction is at an all-time low and why real leadership is so very important today. Rather than wield a cookie cutter, today's leaders must tailor their approach and style to fit the nuances of leading various generations and groups of people without compromising their ideals.

The newest members of the workforce are the Millennials, or so-called Generation Y, who present their own unique challenges. These are people born roughly between 1980 and 2000, and by 2014, they will be 58 million strong. Bosses likely call them the least respectful and most demanding generation yet. Real leaders, on the other hand, recognize that this generation brings tremendous value, skill, and insight to the workplace. Millennials require a different kind of real leadership, one that understands how to corral their energies.

Contrary to bosses' opinions, these "Gen-nexters" are passionate about their work, energetic, and committed, and they're tomorrow's leaders. They will improve American ingenuity, innovation, and competitiveness in an increasingly global marketplace. They're bright, industrious, and driven to succeed; they want to be challenged and given more regular feedback so they can improve. They're technologically savvy, cross-culturally aware, and committed to sustainability and diversity. Millennials are less trusting of corporate titans and politicians. They're also remarkably civic-minded and better equipped to be team-oriented, as a result of changes in our education system that now emphasize team-building and team activities.

The Millennials already boast some great leaders today. Mark Zuckerberg was a computer science student at Harvard

University when he co-founded Facebook in 2004. The company revolutionized social networking. Larry Page and Sergey Brin co-founded Google. Google's head of marketing in the Middle East was Egyptian Wael Ghonim, whose Tweeting about the uprising in Egypt helped act as the catalyst to the revolution that overthrew President Hosni Mubarak. These are the real leaders who dare to have the vision and passion to bring new and radical ideas and approaches to life. Bill Gates and Paul Allen had similar visions and passions when they co-founded Microsoft decades ago.

Non-Traditional Approaches

Millennials gravitate toward organizations that assign them mentors, provide more frequent performance appraisals, give praise for a job well done at the successful conclusion of a project, and offer more flex-time. Non-tradition is the future in the workplace. Employers—big and small—must learn to evolve and embrace a new generation of workers or perish. Forget policies that aren't family-friendly. Penalizing parents for taking time to be with their kids doesn't cut it with this next generation. Neither does the silent treatment in the workplace.

Millennials want to work for companies that have an edge over others. They seek more growth opportunities and speedier advancement than their predecessors did. Thus, organizations that commit the necessary resources to construct their own internal talent engine will more often be selected by this group. It is critically important that businesses motivate the young workforce by closely connecting their jobs—and company success—to career development in a fully integrated way.

Ventura County attorney Michael Bradbury suggests that when it comes to dealing with Millennials, a leader's first step should be to learn all he or she can about them.[8] "The Pew Research Center produced a series of reports on the behaviors, values, and opinions of this group[9] and it is 'must' reading for anyone who supervises or leads people these days," he says.

Unlike the last two generations, Millennials are less trusting of corporations. This provides a golden opportunity to build loyalty toward a company and perhaps results in keeping employees for longer periods with substantial cost savings, says Bradbury:

> Millennials look at loyalty as a two-way street. Leaders today must exhibit a genuine interest in their employees. In a very real sense, they must look at them more as partners than traditional employees. Once a leader understands his people and what motivates them, she or he must adapt the workplace to take maximum advantage of their new way of thinking. This doesn't mean that the business must be run like a collective, but it does mean that they can't proceed in a business-as-usual manner.[10]

Tapping the Value Proposition

Today's young, bright professionals can bring diverse generational points of view to decision-making in business and industry, especially in relation to change dynamics. Too few companies realize that today, too few bosses listen, and as a result companies flounder in the quickly changing global marketplace. Real leaders must look for and listen to what each different generation brings to the workplace table.

Younger generations are often poles apart from older executives in how they approach problems, how they engage in critical thinking, and how they process challenges. Real leaders recognize the differences as positive—as opposed to confrontational—and, in turn, work those different attitudes and approaches into their business and marketing strategies. Because of this, their companies can gain rapid strategic advantages over their competitors.

New generations may not know a specific business, but they understand their generation, what they want, and how they want it. When teamed with the right older mentors, these younger workers can help create a winning team for the business today and for the future.

Listening to Talent

The world of design is fraught with firms who, though successful as artists, rarely possess business acumen. However, Corbin Design, an environmental graphic design firm located in Traverse City, Michigan, has been both, and its leadership's willingness to pay attention to changing markets and marketplace dynamics has paid off. In its 35-year history, Corbin Design has successfully worked in residential and restoration architecture, interior design, and marketing communications, and now specialize in "wayfinding," which is the art of guiding people through complex environments such as medical centers, academic campuses, and cities through signage and other architectural or visual cues. Throughout the firm's trajectory, its leaders have regularly encountered talented designers who grasped participatory roles in the development of the firm, its design process, and client base. Some of that talent succeeded, and some didn't. Corbin Design President Mark VanderKlipp began as a designer, helped build the company to its current status, and, in the process, redefined wayfinding design and put the company miles ahead of its competitors.

As the healthcare industry has transitioned from provider-centered care to patient-centered care, wayfinding has grown in importance in medical facilities. Designers and project managers provide consultative services that focus on the design of healthcare facilities and processes that are more directed toward patients and families. Often, it isn't until wayfinding is discussed as part of a new, proposed building design that it becomes apparent that the location of various services should be changed to better serve the customer. VanderKlipp espouses the idea that "what we do best should make it easier for the next person to do what they do best."[11] In doing so, they change the culture of these organizations while improving access to care.

The Millennial Advantage

Today's Millennials bring different skill sets to the workplace than did previous generations. The reality is that every transformational generation brings its own skill set to the workplace and faces resistance, and when real leaders rise up, change occurs.

What are the positive traits of today's Millennials, and what effect can they have on the workplace? How can you help harness their skills? What can you as a leader do to ensure these younger employees emerge as successful leaders for tomorrow? Why, you may ask, should you bother? The passion, energy, commitment, and creativity that Millennials bring to their work, not to mention their technological savvy, will transform and improve the global marketplace. Leaders who learn how to harness these powerful skills gain an edge on their competition as a result.

Leadership in Tomorrow's Workplace

Growing global marketplaces, evolving technologies, and changing workspaces are major challenges facing tomorrow's leaders. How can a real leader inspire his or her employees if those employees and staff are spread across the city, the state, the country, or even the world? A geographically dispersed workforce already is a reality for many companies, large and small, that have traded their brick-and-mortar office structures for virtual space. Real leaders, though, learn to cope with these new aspects of diversity and manage their companies to excel, in part, by capitalizing on the latest technologies and tools available. They have learned that's essential to remaining competitive.

Leading a remote workforce takes more thought and planning from a communications standpoint. But when done right, a leader becomes more conscious of employees' needs. Out of sight, or off-site, does not mean out of mind.

Big Advantages and Challenges

The Internet age has brought with it many advantages for companies and their leaders who embrace change. The advantages range from lower business expenses to increased flexibility and freedom for employees, and, in many instances, greater creativity and productivity from those employees, too.

However, employees spread across miles and oceans away may not feel connected to or a part of a company. That is where real leaders make the difference. It is inherent in the job of a leader with a geographically diverse workforce to make the effort to meet face-to-face with those employees on a regular basis. Video-conferencing, interactive webinars, and other tools are great for interim communications. But even the most up-to-date technological links cannot replace the personal connection that comes with actual face time. Sitting down with the troops—wherever they are—also can provide a clearer picture of what is really happening in the company and the marketplace. As employee interaction becomes increasingly electronic and distant, companies and their leaders may also have to play bigger and stronger roles as social and community leaders in order to motivate, inspire, and drive the corporate culture.

Blaise Simqu travels the globe—from California to London to Singapore—to keep connected with his company's employees. He is CEO of Sage Publications, an international publisher of journals, books, and e-material for academic, educational, and professional markets. Simqu makes sure the people in his organization—no matter where they are—are heard, involved, and trained to make his company more innovative and to move it forward.

The Hay study cited earlier points to the "flattening" of leadership roles and the increase in team projects—smaller, disparate groups all working toward a primary goal. A positive outgrowth of this team approach is that it may be easier for team members—inherently smaller groups as opposed to an entire workforce—to have actual face time, especially as workforces become more geographically dispersed.

Embracing Change

Despite those demands of the changing workplace, the basics for sustained superior performance fundamentally remain the same. Howdy Holmes of Chelsea Milling wasn't afraid to stand up to past traditions and transform his company from a powerhouse of the past into one of the future. He did so by embracing the past in terms of value to customers and employees, the importance of his employees, and the strength of integrity and character he learned, in part, from his father.

Real leadership implies change—that is, change that moves the organization forward in strategic ways to achieve its overarching goals. Not unlike the promise a brand makes to its constituencies, effective leadership forecasts that needed change will occur and that it will improve the organization's fortunes. It is not enough, however, simply to supply a new vision or new order of things. Real leaders also must help others to grasp change, identify with it, and use it creatively, constructively, and passionately. It must be clear enough to be easily understood but ambiguous enough to stand the test of time and adapt to evolving conditions.

Real leaders must embrace the need for change and their changing roles with it. That means:

- Risking what has become tradition in order to maintain company strengths.
- Developing new policies that balance core traditions with rapidly evolving marketplaces.
- Embracing experimentation and intelligent risk-taking.
- Embracing diversity and finding new ways to touch new audiences.
- Listening to the marketplace en route to finding the right place.

Making It Work Today

In today's global, 24/7 economy, leaders must learn to connect with their employees, on-site and off, in different, and often more visible, ways. As with Simqu of Sage Publications, a CEO or team leader must spend more time visiting with employees in far-off places. That means meeting in large, as well as small, groups, and then eliciting and listening to ideas, suggested improvements, and concerns. A "suggestion box" isn't enough, either. Real leaders make time for real communication.

It is essential that a leader fully understand the needs of his or her people in order to maximize success on the job. Unlike his or her traditional in-house counterpart, a geographically distant leader does not have the opportunity for daily, in-person observations to make sure everything runs smoothly. Staff must have the right work environment with the right equipment to do the job. That includes the latest possible technological tools that make it easier to stay connected. In addition, leaders of a disparate workforce shoulder the inherent responsibility of making very sure that employees and middle managers—in-house or remote—clearly understand stated goals, strategies, expectations, and assignments.

The Human Side

The best leaders also genuinely connect with employees by showing their human side. Leadership, after all, is about relationships with others, and those relationships are essential to promote workplace culture and strengthen trust, which, in turn, increases productivity. Real leaders pay attention to employees' human needs, too.

Other important aspects of leading successfully in today's evolving workspaces include:

- ◆ Adapting to differing demands or varied meetings that cross time zones. For example, one meeting may be an important special event celebrating a team's recent success, and the next meeting might be a very challenging encounter with investors, both involving participants across different time zones.

- ◆ Maintaining what Simqu refers to as "calendar integrity"—doing what you say you'll do when you say you'll do it. Too many CEOs scratch meetings with employees at the last minute because the previous meeting ran longer than expected. That kind of disregard can quickly erode employee trust, because it conveys the strong message the employee is less important to the leader than other audiences.

- ◆ Drafting your major messages yourself instead of turning the responsibility over to speechwriters or assistants. Once the message is established, at least in the form of ideas and a first draft, it may then be appropriate to hand it off to an expert or assistant to finalize.

- ◆ Ensuring human resource staff are effective com-municators and know how to work with employees off-site and on. Too many HR types don't know the difference and often are ineffective in working with employees off-site, especially when it comes to tech-nology. IT staff need to be effective communicators, too, when remote or off-site workers are involved.

- ◆ Being tech-savvy. Real leaders today—young, old, and in between—must learn to capitalize on all the communication means they have available, includ-ing social media such Twitter and Facebook, tex-ting, Skype, and other teleconferencing methods. Leaders must take advantage of all this to stay in touch with employees, markets, communities, and key constituencies. As part of that, it is also essen-tial to know the preferred forms of communication for immediate staff.

- ◆ Ensuring that both remote and in-house employees receive the training they need to utilize these new technologies.

- ◆ Being sure communications expectations and stan-dards are clear and set up front. Don't leave re-sponse times to chance. Make certain everyone is on the same page as to how he or she is required to communicate with the home office and the leader, how often, and what feedback is required.

Leadership Lessons From the Marines

When we think of the military, we often imagine cam-ouflage-clad soldiers on patrol amid the dust of Iraq or Afghanistan, rolling across the desert in caravans of Humvees. Hollywood movie images of military leadership are often overly macho and violent, and oversimplify the leadership principles that are practiced throughout the military's complex missions around the world.

Crucial Ideals

Hollywood overlooks the core tenets of leadership in the Corps—truisms very much at home and a must to emulate in the corporate battlefields of today's global marketplace. Business leaders, like the Marines, must be adaptive, take risks, operate frugally, demonstrate courage of conviction, discipline, and inspire employees. For good reason, the University of Pennsylvania's prestigious Wharton School integrates the Marines' leadership lessons into its management curriculum. Wharton's MBA students visit Marine Corps Base Quantico in Virginia to listen, observe, actively participate in, and experience a special "boot camp," and learn from real leaders.

For nearly two years I worked almost daily with Marines. Here are six of the Marines' most important leadership crucibles that high-performance organizations and real leaders must emulate:

1. Consistently deliver results. Display an unshakable "can do" attitude and relentless passion to exceed the goal.

2. Live out the mottos "Lead, follow, or get out of the way" and "Never quit."

3. Exhibit an enduring service culture characterized by acting above one's own interests; a fiercely proud tradition of honor, discipline, and humility; and a promise never to leave anyone behind.

4. Assume a state of constant readiness. This demands remarkable adaptiveness and perseverance, a trained flexibility to overcome any obstacle, and

the ability to do more with fewer resources than others.

5. Provide leadership that is consistent, transparent, and reaches toward a higher standard for the organization. The leader should "carry the torch" and serve as a paragon of inspiration to the troops.

6. Live out the motto to "be no better friend," unafraid of admitting shortcomings and always committed to making it right.

Retired USMC Maj. Gen. Leslie M. Palm, former president and CEO of Marine Corps Association & Foundation, and former director for Marine Corps Staff, Headquarters Marine Corps, Washington, D.C., is a prime example of a real leader whose dedication to the Marine leadership crucibles has inspired others around him for many years. Palm is a decorated combat veteran of the Vietnam War and Operations Desert Storm and Desert Shield. Despite his accomplishments, he is humble, modest, thoughtful, and steady. He is the same person today in terms of his values and strength of character that he was 50 years ago as a high school student in Marysville, California. Les Palm and I have been friends since boyhood; we grew up a block apart in California. Les was our high school student body president and an excellent athlete. He went on to play football for the University of Oregon. Even in those early years he had that unique sense of team and the ability to remain calm under pressure. During our summers in college, Les would spend a few weeks with the U.S. Marines as part of their Platoon Leaders Class, where he began to show an increasing sense of self-confidence, but never arrogance. Anyone who knew him knew he would succeed at anything he did.

Courageous Conviction

Real leaders manifest courage of conviction in their willingness to stand up for their ideals, their employees, and their company and products. Discipline and conviction like Palm's is an expectation that permeates the Marine Corps. It is also a requirement for leadership success in today's workplace. Taking any business into unchartered waters—as with leading a force into combat—is not for the meek; neither is competing with fierce competitors with stronger brands or launching new products in a crowded market.

Retired U.S. Marine Gen. Anthony C. "Tony" Zinni is another leader who understands the importance of having the courage and audacity to speak out when something is wrong. Among his many accomplishments, Zinni is a former commander in chief of the U.S. Central Command at the Pentagon, a past U.S. Peace Envoy to the Middle East, Special Envoy to the Henri Dunant Centre for Humanitarian Dialogue (Indonesia, Philippines, and Sudan peace efforts), and chairman of the board of the multi-billion-dollar conglomerate BAE Systems, Inc.

As Gen. Zinni has exemplified throughout his decorated and honored career, audacity, courage, and boldness are essential traits for a real leader. The general is his own man, candid and anything but an ideologue. He was pointedly blunt in criticizing President George W. Bush's national security team for their lack of post-war planning and for failing to fully understand Iraqi society. As an astute leadership expert, Zinni believes the old definitions of leadership must be changed.

Leaders must be willing to speak out when the situation calls for change—whether internally in a business, or externally, relating to the community and beyond. That doesn't mean leaders are resident critics. Instead, they carefully and thoughtfully choose the right time and place to speak out when something is not right. Leaders must be prepared for criticism and threats of disloyalty, too. But they must meanwhile stay the course, remaining true to their ideals, employees, and businesses even when confronted with criticism.

Bosses Can Become Leaders

As reflected in the outstanding actions of the individuals you have just read about, real leadership can and does bring about change. Real leadership is not always the fastest and shortest route, but it's definitely the most long-lasting and successful. Bosses can be transformed into leaders; like almost anyone else, they, too, can learn the right way to lead. A shift in attitude is the first step—from a domineering boss to a consensus-building leader.

If you strive to be a leader and not a boss, remember and subscribe to these values and practices:

- Commit to driving fear out of your organization.
- Drive out other negative attitudes that undermine performance and morale.
- Strengthen your corporate culture with discipline and compassion.
- Believe in and build up your people.
- Give clear assignments.
- Be available when needed.
- Listen attentively.
- Display high integrity in everything you do.

You Can Do It, Too

You, too, can become a great leader by connecting with your employees. Some actions that can help entrench and enrich your leadership include:

- Learning to shift gears quickly if necessary.

- Doing what you say you will do when it comes to employees. If you promise to do something, follow through and follow up.

- Not allowing others to draft your major messages. The voice of a communication must be from the leader.

- Being sure your staff members are effective communicators, too.

- Being tech-savvy and not afraid to use technology to your advantage. That goes for social networks such as Facebook and Twitter, too.

- Giving your employees and staff the tools and the training they need.

- Setting specific standards for interaction/communication between employees, staff, and leaders.

Takeaway

- Philanderers, racists, bullies, and egomaniacs with anger-management problems have no place in today's workplace, especially among the ranks of leaders. Not only do they undermine employee morale, but they also sabotage a business's success.

- Real leaders must pay attention to the personal needs of their employees. Real leaders create a work environment—a climate or culture, if you will—that enables their associates to flourish.

- Millennials bring unique and outstanding talents to the workplace. Real leaders must learn how to tap into those talents.

- The 21st-century global marketplace requires an evolution of leadership strategies. With businesses operating 24/7 and across nations and the world, leaders must stay connected to their employees by every high-tech and traditional means possible, from social media to face-to-face visits.

- Business leaders would do well to emulate the U.S. Marines' high standards of conduct, including traits such as the ability to adapt and the willingness to take risks, operate frugally, demonstrate courageous conviction, discipline, and inspire employees.

- Today's leaders must be willing to take their businesses into uncharted waters in order to reap big rewards.

- Bosses can learn to be leaders, and it starts with a willingness to shift one's attitude from domination to consensus-building.

Chapter 3

Real Leaders Communicate

*Electric communication will never be a substitute for the
face of someone who with their soul encourages
another person to be brave and true.*

—Charles Dickens

The ability to communicate effectively is one of the most important ingredients for a real leader. Yet true and honest communication has fast become a lost art in today's digital age. Instead, it has been replaced by high-tech devices and third-party mouthpieces that actually derail real interaction, and fuel the demise of communication. How many CEOs—or anyone else, for that matter—write for themselves, or make time for face-to-face contact with subordinates or even an old-fashioned telephone call? Even if CEOs do meet with employees and managers, how many actually listen? The answer today is not many.

In our global, plugged-in, tuned-in, digital age, face time may seem a bit unwieldy. However, face-to-face meetings as well as communiqués and speeches written firsthand are proven techniques for effective communication by real leaders.

This is the "e-age" for communication: we have software templates, texting and instant messaging technologies, ghost-writers, PR experts, and downsizing experts all acting in the name of time-saving efficiencies. Even multi-million-dollar deals come down to back-and-forth texting between executives, with the lawyers and accountants left to work out the details later.

These days, a top-level executive may have occasional meetings or even regularly scheduled get-togethers with high-level staff to discuss company matters. But in how many of those meetings does he or she give undivided attention or demonstrate a genuine interest about what's being said? Not many. And, when it comes to a CEO actually writing his or her own communications, you would be hard-pressed trying to find one. Again, bosses are many; leaders are few.

Using all stand-in communication is wrong, as is using all digital—whether it is talk, Tweets, blogs, video-conferencing, or statements written by third parties. Although plenty of top executives have the requisite blogs, and still more Tweet, few write their own content, whether it's blogs, Webpage greetings, presentations, letters to the editor, or messages to shareholders. Today's executives rely too often on their in-house or outsourced public relations team, legal department, administrative assistants, or external consultants to draft their formal documents as well as their brief notes. According to London's *Financial Times* international poll of 750 executive bloggers, only two of 10 senior business executives actually write their own blog posts.[1] Noel M. Tichy, noted author, professor of management and organizations at the University of Michigan's Ross School of Business, and former director of the GE Leadership Development Center in Crotonville, paints an even more dismal picture of today's communication disconnect: "Ninety percent of CEOs have someone else write for them."[2] Relying on the excuse "I'm too busy," or perhaps "I'm too important," the corporate world has lost the art of communication.

Not every chief executive subscribes to the philosophy of diminished discussion. Some strive for more, even though this often involves herculean, time-consuming efforts on their part. Blaise Simqu of Sage Publications is a chief executive who regularly connects with the people in his organization—no matter where they are. A firm believer in personally modeling the behavior he expects from his employees, Simqu also recognizes the importance of being home on weekends with his family. That is a real leader. Who would not want to work for a leader who preaches and practices balance for himself and his associates?

In the public sector, where real talk is rare, U.S. Federal Reserve Chairman Ben Bernanke held his first press conference on April 27, 2011. Actually it was the *first ever* press conference by a Federal Reserve chairman. Bernanke may not have said anything new in his landmark appearance, but it was an unprecedented step toward more communication, not less.

Whether or not an executive believes in real communication, it can and does net important results. If you communicate and connect with employees, no matter how volatile an issue or situation, any confrontation is manageable, and outcomes will be more successful.

The Art of Connection

Make the effort to know your audience, the competition, and your adversaries, and outcomes likely will be more consistent and predictable. Robert Laverty, former president and CEO of St. Joseph Mercy Hospital System based in Ann Arbor, Michigan, was never arrogant or cruel, but always modest. He was self-confident without being cocky, and he not only knew how to connect, but he also understood the value of communication. I worked with him, and one late afternoon at the hospital, I met with him just prior to a meeting he had scheduled with the medical staff. The meeting was to discuss an important strategic opportunity for the hospital, and Laverty wanted medical staff support for the plan. Up until that point, doctors had indicated their concern about the pace of change—too much new building and too many plans to build new facilities and establish new programs. I asked Laverty if he was worried about his ability to persuade the medical staff to embrace his plan. He responded, "If I can't convince them, I don't deserve to be in this job."

Laverty knew that the impending discussions would likely be heated, but he also understood how to communicate and connect with physicians. He knew he could deliver. A master communicator, he prevailed in that meeting. The hospital's medical staff embraced the changes, and Laverty, the medical staff, the hospital, and the community ended up winning with the resulting expansion plans.

Bob Laverty exhibited leadership traits that are the lore of management books. He had an incomparable ability to conceive and articulate a vision. He could "see" into the future of the organization and plan effectively to succeed in that future. And, he knew how to charm others into pursuing his visions. He understood that no vision will reach fruition if it is not shared and owned by the team charged with executing it.

Laverty also understood what management gurus such as W. Edwards Deming and Sakichi Toyoda knew: the importance of management by literally walking around. I recall clearly the first time he suggested I accompany him to one of the patient floors in the hospital. He was the first CEO who taught me the importance of visiting the patient units at different times of the day and night to get to know the staff, to better understand their challenges and the special calling inherent in working in a healthcare setting. In many ways, he understood both patient and staff needs and how best to meet them. The esteemed Northwestern University professor Phillip Kotler would surely have called him one of the best marketers in the entire healthcare field as Laverty understood both the art and science of the profession.

Another superb communicator and leader I encountered during my first years in Ann Arbor was the vice president of academic affairs at the University of Michigan, Allan Smith. I probably learned more from him than anyone else I have ever worked for. He was genuine, humble, and unpretentious, and he always had time for others. My first encounter with him is a testament to that.

Shortly after arriving at the University of Michigan to pursue my doctoral degree, my wife, Joan, and I were walking across Regents Plaza in front of the administration building as Smith and university president Robben Fleming walked out. At the time, we had no idea who they were. We must have appeared lost because both men smiled at us, stopped to introduce themselves, and asked us if they could help us. After I introduced myself as a doctoral student who had just arrived from Pomona College in Claremont, California, Smith offered to meet with me in his office to see if he could be of any help. It didn't matter that we were strangers; this real leader openly and without hesitancy took the time and offered to make more time for someone else. From that chance encounter, I spent the next year as a staff assistant to Smith.

I received a priceless education observing how a great leader has extreme patience. Despite a blistering schedule, Smith always made time for those who sought his counsel. He literally gave 100 percent of his attention to the person or persons he was with at the time. No matter what, he never became angry or vindictive; he never appeared ruffled and was always genuinely pleasant, polite, and kind. He could and did charm everyone with this incredible warmth, intelligence, and undivided attention.

As Smith, Fleming, Laverty, and other real leaders understand, real leadership requires real, live communication, not the texted, Tweeted, or e-mailed thoughts, words, or interpretations by someone else in your name. An e-communication is often necessary, but expressing your own thoughts and ideas in face-to-face, honest, two-way talk—body language and all— overshadows its poor unemotional cousin.

Former Dow employee Jerry Benson related the following anecdote from his tenure at Dow Chemical: "Leland Doan, as president of Dow Chemical, when he would walk by a management employee in the hallway, would often ask, 'How's business today?'" That simple question, posed in a casual way, forced the employee to measure his or her current situation in terms of both past and future goals. More important, coming from the company's leader, the question reinforced a personal connection and commitment on the part of the leader as well as the employee. It's a great question to ask yourself daily—and those around you if you are in a leadership role.

Write It Yourself

Real leaders author their own thoughts. Sure, they may have a bit of help from an assistant or a PR expert to refine their work, but the thoughts, direction, approach, and attitude of real leaders belong to them. They write their messages, period. Admiral Zumwalt may not have written the final copy for his "Z-grams," but you can bet that he had plenty of input on the ideas, approach, and attitude expressed in each of them.

Consider a few advantages for someone in a leadership role writing his or her own communications:

- CEOs formulate and chart strategic direction for an organization. Translating those thoughts into writing or organizing them for personal interaction sharpens their focus, lessens confusion and rework, increases the trust of others, inspires followership, and improves outcomes.

- Putting thoughts in writing forces leaders to be clear, concise, and cogent. Former Secretary of State and Chairman of the Joint Chiefs of Staff, Army Gen. Colin Powell said: "Successful leaders know how to define their mission, convey it to their subordinates...."[3]

- Real leaders are also teachers. Part of the teaching process means writing down your thoughts first, then sharing them, inviting feedback, and discussing alternative ideas. Writing helps clarify your vision while it increases your credibility as a leader. CEOs who write the first drafts of their major messages are much more likely to rally stakeholders in ways no speechwriter can imitate.

Real Leaders Know How to Listen

The business world has no shortage of heroes past or present. These are individuals whose visions and personal values form the fabric of their missions, and help make their people great leaders and their companies hugely successful. These people are heroes who personify their values and pay attention to what others say and do. They listen to employees, to customers, and to the markets.

We've all worked for or with, or heard about, the boss who's impossible to contact. Yet every one of the real leaders you have or will read about in these pages regularly mingles and mixes with, talks to, and learns from those who are nearby. Bosses lock themselves away in their "ivory towers," isolated from those around them; real leaders do not. That communication creates an essential awareness and connection with the company, employees, and the community that helps ensure success. It should be standard operating procedure for all levels of leadership.

Regularly connecting and networking with others in your organization—and not only in your job strata—helps build long-term alliances and provides valuable feedback for the short and long term. If you are a CEO or executive, that means taking the time to interact with your staff and your customers. Outside the workplace, the key is being perceptive and receptive to others, and sometimes both work and leisure spaces overlap.

Not every leader needs to be a globetrotter, but all real leaders do need to listen and be accessible. During my administrative tenures with various hospital systems, I always made a point to join doctors and nurse executives on their rounds. I did so not because I had to, but because it was a way to talk with physicians, nurses, and health professionals, and to experience the hospital both day and night. I wanted to get to know all the people working in the facility and to understand their concerns, challenges, families, issues, and problems. A hospital is a 24/7 operation, and its employees and medical staff may have different concerns depending on their shifts. The night shift is less distracted by the day's activities, and night workers generally can better focus on the job at hand.

This kind of communication helped me do a better job. For example, when it was my turn to serve as the nighttime on-call administrator and something extraordinary came up, I knew what was going on, who was involved, and who I could depend on to help get the problem or issue solved. My visibility in and knowledge of a particular facility day and night also boosted my credibility as a representative of the hospital in the community. To truly represent the business, you must truly know the business—and that means both its day and night operations.

Similarly, administrators at Miami Valley Hospital in Dayton, Ohio, were required to spend one day a month "on the floor" assisting patients and their families, medical staff, and support personnel. Such hands-on involvement led to an administrative team that was truly in touch with the ongoing issues of the facility.

Driving Success

You may be the best leader in the world—or at least think you are—but if you can't enlist others in the effort, true success will prove elusive.

When I became chief of public relations and marketing for Indiana University Medical Center in Indianapolis, I used lessons in interpersonal dynamics to transform communications and create more open cooperation throughout our facilities. At the time, the medical center was typical of most academic medical campuses—the *modus operandi* was toleration between "us and them." Doctors and staff, executives and boards did their jobs but often did not work closely with others. As a leader, I listened when and where others had not, and the efforts paid off. Most of the 300 physicians and staff ended up routinely involved in marketing, branding, and affiliation outreach initiatives, which were highly successful. Without that buy-in and expertise among the different constituencies, I doubt we would have had the substantial successes we achieved.

Real listening involves an acute awareness of what is happening and changing in the workplace and in life. Further still, a leader is willing to embrace the needs—personal and professional—that those changes demand.

R. Duke Blackwood, director of the Ronald Reagan Presidential Library in Simi Valley, California, is a highly approachable and expert communicator. Because of those skills, positive changes come about. He's a brilliant fundraiser, highly innovative in program development, and enormously skilled in developing relationships with business and academia, world and national leaders, schoolchildren and teachers. His "Team Reagan" approach created an environment for his staff to succeed as a team, more than doubling the Library's attendance since President Reagan's death, developing award-winning education programs, and dramatically increasing the Library's visibility. Today, the Simi Valley library is the most visited of our nation's presidential libraries.

Personal and Personable

The late Fred Meijer was president and CEO of Meijer, which began as a small Greenville, Michigan–based grocery and household goods store founded by his father. He was renowned for knowing the names of all his employees and customers, and greeted them by name. Meijer recognized the connection that comes with personal communication. Even as his family's superstore empire grew, Meijer continued to maintain that connection until his retirement, when he still would occasionally greet customers and employees, and collect carts in store parking lots.

Today, Meijer is still family owned, and has more than 190 locations throughout Michigan, Ohio, Indiana, Illinois, and Kentucky. The company follows its original mantra: "Take care of your customers, team members, and community...and all of them will take care of you, just like a family."

Another great leader, statesman, creative thinker, eloquent speaker, and tireless crusader for college students is David L. Warren, PhD. He clearly recognizes and understands the importance of connecting with those around him. He also knows that true leadership is about making others better as a result of your presence and making sure your impact endures in your absence. Today he is a tireless advocate for private education funding on Capitol Hill as president of the National Association of Independent Colleges and Universities, a Washington, D.C.–based industry group. He's also a former president of Ohio Wesleyan University, a former alderman and chief administrative officer for the City of New Haven, Connecticut, a former Assistant Secretary of Yale University, and a graduate of Washington State University, Yale, and the University of Michigan.

When Warren assumed the presidency of Ohio Wesleyan University in the 1980s, times were tough. Alumni relations were less than ideal, behavior at campus fraternities was an issue, fundraising was down, and relations with the local community and the surrounding area were somewhat strained. Warren's university-owned home was not yet ready for him and his family of five, so he opted to live in one of the university's residence halls. It was a brilliant move that cemented positive relations with everyone. He used the dorm room to meet students and staff informally. This story made national headlines and immediately endeared the new president to students, faculty, alumni, and townspeople. In fact, living in the dorm was such a positive experience, Warren established an intergenerational living community at the school that thrives today, 20 years later, and remains part of his legacy of leadership.

For those aspiring leaders who doubt the power of personal and real communication, the next time you're out of the office, try this simple experiment: smile at the next few people you see and pay attention to how each responds; chances are good that the majority of people will smile back. Try the same experiment in your workplace and see the results. Start personally communicating with those around you. Your relationship with them likely will change.

Put Tweets and IMs Aside

Electronic communication is integral to today's business world, but think about cutting back on the Tweets and instant messages (IMs), and avoid relying on e-mail for all your communications. Instead, try to approach projects and problem-solving in your office with the same face-to-face openness and willingness to communicate that you demonstrated in your smile experiment. Such personal interaction can produce positive ideas and results, especially in an up-and-down economic environment.

Nearly everyone can recall an instance involving back-and-forth e-mails with someone in the workplace or elsewhere that involved a misjudged cue, misunderstood content, or missed opportunity. The e-mail "oops" could be nothing more than a misunderstood punch line for a joke. But on a more sobering note, if the e-mail exchange is in the workplace context, and the misunderstanding is something such as an insult or involves taking the wrong action that results in a negative outcome, the consequences can be far more serious.

Never allow e-mail to completely replace in-person communication. E-mailing, texting, and Tweeting cannot convey the personal and important nuances and critical thought processes of telephone discussions and face-to-face meetings. Anyone who thinks they can has not yet learned this lesson the hard way.

Do take advantage of the benefits of high-tech communications; just use them properly, and don't rely on them as the only form of "face-to-face" communication. Video-conferences, for example, can be a cohesive tool for project teams, or an e-mail or a Tweet can be valuable to convey a real-time confirmation.

These communication tools are valuable as ancillaries, as long as they're not used as a replacement for more direct, personal communication.

Concrete Results

Warren netted great results from interaction, collaboration, and face-to-face communication—not only laying the foundation for his tenure at Ohio Wesleyan, but for success in the community as well, and later at the national level at the NAICU (National Association of Independent Colleges and Universities) in Washington, D.C.

McDonald's Ray Kroc was a leader in fostering communication, cooperation, and innovation from his franchisees. His business model was a three-legged stool that stood strong because everyone interacted and recognized the importance of each leg: franchises owned by franchisees, McDonald's corporate, and McDonald's suppliers. Along the way, Kroc fostered tremendous innovation from the field: three of McDonald's most popular menu items—the Big Mac, Egg McMuffin, and Filet-o-Fish—were invented by franchisees.[4] (Incidentally, one of my most enjoyable and rewarding learning experiences was serving on the founding board of the West Michigan Ronald McDonald House in Grand Rapids, Michigan and spending time at McDonald's University in Oak Brook, Ill.)

Taking Stock of Your Communication Skills

Your communication should be up close and personal, and it should be authentic. Why should you or any leader need to turn over speeches and other important communiqués to speechwriters, public relations specialists, or their assistants? The answer is, you and they shouldn't. There's no good reason for it, especially with so many electronic programs available today to facilitate effective writing and outlining. For example, the iA

Writer for the iPad is a simple and intuitive word-processing system that helps most anyone write down their thoughts at least in an outline or draft form.

The writing process may be difficult for you as an untrained writer, because it involves organization and evolution of ideas. But it's an important step. When, as a leader or aspiring leader, you plot strategy or determine policies, if you draft the content yourself, the end result is more focused, better thought through, clearer, and more concise. Outcomes are further improved, too, because the personal connection fosters employee trust and followership.

Why should real leaders still rely on physical connections and communications? We as leaders must use every method available today to stay connected and in touch with employees, the community, our customers, and markets. If we do not, the disconnection becomes a real threat to our company's success.

Real leaders must go the extra mile to ensure connections with their teams and employees or lose touch. But that does not mean leaders should not also employ every other high-tech means possible to enhance that communication. That includes social media such as Twitter and Facebook, Websites, e-mails, instant messaging, and texting, plus traditional communication methods such as snail mail, paper handouts, faxes, and the like. The goal of your communication strategy should not be "going paperless" for its own sake, but establishing real and direct back-and-forth interaction between leaders, their employees, their managers, and the community, and getting it right in order to remain competitive. In today's marketplace, there's no reason for coming up short on communication.

How could the leaders in your life communicate more efficiently and effectively combining both e-methods and traditional communication tools? What can you do to communicate more effectively and efficiently in your own life? What's stopping you from doing it?

You Can Do It, Too

Not only does face-to-face communication convey real connections, it can give you as a leader a better understanding of what's really happening in your workplace and in the marketplace. Use face time to complement extensive electronic communication and the more traditional forms such as faxes, printouts, and notes to give your company and employees the competitive edge.

As a leader, set up a company Facebook page and a blog to chat business and develop ideas with your staff; and Tweet the newest to stay connected with your employees and staff, too. Listen to what others have to say and be open to different viewpoints. Use e-mail, a note, and/or a bulletin board post to follow up, and then a face-to-face meeting to go over ideas and make sure everyone is in the loop. All these types of communication can help build that all-important genuine sense of community and an environment in which people want to work together. Remember: real leaders listen to all views, respect all parties, and then embark forward on a journey to make a difference.

Takeaway

- Face-to-face communication enables leaders to really connect with employees and to better understand what's happening in the workplace.

- Social media, e-mails, texting, and instant messaging do have a place in the workplace as long as they are not the only form of back-and-forth communication.

- If a leader connects and communicates with his or her staff, confrontations or divisive issues generally end up less volatile, and it's easier to reach a consensus.

- Real leaders know how to use humor to diffuse and to reassure.

- Writing your own messages helps you clarify your vision and chart your strategic direction.

- Real leaders need to learn how to listen to their employees, their markets, and their communities.

- Connecting and networking with others—no matter their job strata—can help develop long-term, important alliances.

Chapter 4

Real Leaders Have a Unique Make-Up

Passion rebuilds the world for the youth. It makes all things alive and significant.

—Ralph Waldo Emerson

Leadership is not about the size of someone's paycheck or the length of his or her resume; it is about passion, guts, and the willingness to give back. Too often people confuse the need and desire to manage (boss) others or the craving to get rich with passion and guts. On the surface, these characteristics can appear similar. But closer examination quickly reveals how far apart they are when it comes to action, attitude, and reality. Bosses bully, whereas real leaders inspire by passion and guts, and rally those around them to follow and achieve greatness. Of course, we can't prove it scientifically, but it almost seems as if there's a "leadership make-up"—if not in the genes, then an alignment of certain traits that, if developed properly, can allow someone to flourish as a leader.

Passion: The Starting Point

Passion in many forms surrounds us every day. But little of it translates into real business or community leadership that commits to helping companies, employees, and others so that everyone benefits from it. The brand of passion that infuses great leaders needs to be "fervor." It is an infectious lifestyle that includes living one's ideals, having a clear vision for the future, and possessing a mindset that enables the achievement of success in the face of adversity. For individuals who have found their passion, invariably life becomes more exciting, rewarding, and enjoyable, too. In the workplace, that passion translates into creation of a strong corporate culture that can help drive an organization's success in good times and bad. Look around you at those companies that have remained strong through the current recession. Somewhere in their make-up there is probably a passionate, real leader.

Passion is the best form of PR and fuels the perception by others that a leader is, indeed, just that. People want to know that their leaders—in government, business, church, sports, and elsewhere—fervently ascribe to what they say. They want to know that their leaders' views will not be easily swayed or vanish mysteriously when times get tough. People want to believe that the actions of their leaders are motivated by a strong sense of purpose and by values encased in passion. Above all, leaders must lead by example, teach others how to lead, be willing to always extend a helping hand to people in need, and always be humble and compassionate in how they approach life.

The Power of Belief

Tom Monaghan, founder of Domino's Pizza, has had an enormously successful career. But he certainly didn't start out that way. His father died when Tom was 4 years old; his mother couldn't take care of him and his brother, so Monaghan ended up in an orphanage and foster homes. He dropped out of college and initially failed at the pizza business. But he was driven to succeed and passionately convinced that his vision of pizza delivered fast and fresh for a reasonable price would fly. So he kept trying, listened and learned from others, and finally got it right. We all know the rest as home-delivery history.

Comebacks in organizational and political life are the stuff of legends. Americans identify with those who have been knocked down and bounce back to experience success. Many of Tom Monaghan's critics made the mistake of writing him off when he lost his pizza business. He has been variously described as wacky, grandiose, over-zealous, lowbrow, heavy-handed, and worse. I liked him, though, the very first time I met him, probably attracted to his "comeback-kid" quality. He tasted failure several times in business, only to rise triumphantly, surpassing nearly everyone's expectations.

Another leader who tackles his responsibilities with purposeful zeal and incredible passion that transfers to others is U.S. Senator Dan Coats, who has served in both the House of Representatives and Senate on and off for more than three decades. He's been honored for his impassioned leadership by various organizations. I ran head-on into that passion-in-action while working as head of marketing and public relations for Indiana University Medical Center and also serving on Sen. Coats's Naval Academy Selection Committee. Some Congressmen turn the military academies' selection process into something political or just another task that must be done—but not Sen. Coats. This was a responsibility handed to him by his position and entrusted to him by the voters in Indiana, and he was passionate that it be done right. He absolutely wanted to identify the most qualified and deserving candidates to attend the academies. That was the charge, and that's what we did under Coats's leadership.

Standout athletes personify the "belief" factor, and some become great leaders in the community and in business. Former *Boston Globe* assistant sports editor, and more recently retired *Ventura County Star* sports editor, Larry Ames singles out quarterback Doug Flutie as "the biggest leader on the field of play" that he has ever observed. Flutie was relatively small in stature, 5-feet, 9-inches tall, yet he was a mountain among others, on and off the field. He believed in himself, his athletic abilities, and his leadership capabilities. He took calculated gambles essential to his team's success, and he didn't waver. Ames recounts a bit about Flutie's resolve and skill:

> Flutie...wasn't highly recruited (out of high school) and went to Boston College as a defensive back. Flutie went up to Boston College football coach Jack Bicknell and asked if he could be put on the quarterback depth chart if he had a strong showing in the annual Shriners' Football Classic being played at Boston College. Flutie performed well and Bicknell kept his promise, placing Flutie fourth on the quarterback depth chart.
>
> In Flutie's freshman year, Boston College was struggling, as it usually did against Penn State. Already, two of the four BC quarterbacks had been injured and the third-string quarterback was performing poorly. Bicknell decided to give Flutie a chance. Flutie rallied BC for a touchdown before halftime and nearly pulled off the victory in the fourth period.
>
> Flutie started every game for the rest of his career, winning the Heisman Trophy in his senior year.... Flutie became a Hall of Fame quarterback in the Canadian Football League and played for a few NFL teams before retiring at age 43 with the New England Patriots.
>
> In the 2005 season finale against the Miami Dolphins, Flutie made a drop kick, the first in the NFL since 1941. It was a fitting ending to a storied career.[1]

Off the football field, Flutie is a real leader, too. He and his wife, Laurie, founded the Doug Flutie, Jr. Foundation for Autism after their son was diagnosed with the disease at age 3. The foundation awards grants to nonprofit organizations that provide services for children with autism and to organizations that conduct research on the causes and effects of autism. Since 1998, the Fluties have helped raise more than $11 million for autism.[2]

Roots of Passion

For some, passion is rooted in life's experiences. History is filled with stories about the kindling of a fervent flame—from the politician exposed to the plight of those less fortunate, to the college student encountering a professor who taps into something buried deep inside. Passion can be instilled at a young age, the result of parental modeling, and the discussions and decisions that shape a childhood environment. It is the same with other important lessons, such as the value of hard work and of not giving up in the face of adversity.

Leadership can be in the genes, too, waiting to be developed. For me, it started with the "family business." My grandfather, father, and uncles were strong community leaders and instilled in me that sense of purpose. My mother was a schoolteacher and hospital volunteer who introduced me to the importance of looking deeper within the individual and treating everyone with respect. With those foundations, I was able to watch, listen, and learn from those around me; build on experiences from supervisors, leaders, fellow workers, and beyond; and develop the concept of a real leader. I had great teachers, too—role models who made a big difference in my life and in the lives of others. Even without parents or grandparents, uncles, or siblings as role models, it is possible to harness your passions, learn how to lead others, and then excel as a real leader.

Passion and Commitment Work in Tandem

Positive passion and commitment surround us every day in the form of teachers who care, nurses who go the extra mile, pastors who reach out, neighbors who want to make their community a better place to live, and other individuals who deeply care and willingly volunteer. Too little of this passion, though, translates into real leadership committed to helping companies, employees, and communities come out winners.

One leader who does fit the dynamic and whose corporate and civic accomplishments demonstrate his commitment is Limoneira's Edwards. His vision helped him lead his company back to its roots of stewardship of the land and the community. Working with Limoneira's rich assets and community buy-in, Limoneira is achieving an enviable sustainability—long-term success for all parties. "Part of sustainability is that you have to take care of your workforce. Our people are our great asset," says Edwards. To that end, the company worked in partnership with its nearby community, Santa Paula, California, and developed a community master plan for growth and long-term success.[3]

Judith Rodin, president of the University of Pennsylvania from 1994 to 2004, and current president of the Rockefeller Foundation, is another great leader whose passion helps the world around her in lasting ways. "I believe for a university to be truly world class it needs to do great, visible things in its own backyard," she said while still at Penn. Under her leadership and fueled by her passion, the university has become a beacon in its own backyard. Among her accomplishments was revitalization of the West Philadelphia neighborhood around the university. Rodin also oversaw a meteoric rise in student applications, research grants, new faculty, and fundraising as well as leaps in reputation—all major markers by which universities are measured.[4] Marc H. Morial, president and CEO of the National Urban League, had this to say about Rodin and her accomplishments at Pennsylvania:

At a time when many urban academic institutions raised fences and erected buildings with forbidding walls to protect their staff and students from encroaching crime, the University of Pennsylvania and President Judith Rodin questioned how this approach would benefit the institution in the long run. Rodin's account of the university's ground-breaking initiatives to embrace and reinvigorate the surrounding neighborhood shows how anchor institutions must operate in the 21st century if they are to remain competitive.[5]

When Steven Sample took over as president of the University of Southern California in 1991, the school was a sports giant, but its academic reputation didn't measure up to its athletic prowess. With legendary zeal and passion, he set about transforming the school into an equally strong academic institution. His efforts and success at doing so are renowned, as is the fact that he was a forerunner in forming alliances and partnerships with communities to revitalize neighborhoods around college campuses. Along the way, he teamed with leadership guru Warren Bennis to teach a course on leadership at the university, and together they coauthored *A Contrarian's Guide to Leadership* (Jossey-Bass, 2001). When announcing his plans to retire in August 2010, Sample said:

> For Kathryn and me, the presidency of USC has been far more than just a job. It has been a calling, an all-consuming passion to move this university ahead farther and faster than any other university in the United States. We have been blessed to have pursued this mission in the company of many colleagues and friends who share our commitment to USC's advancement. Our years here have simply been exhilarating.[6]

Passion and commitment lead to transformation and excellence—one of the leadership lessons from Kenneth Beachler.

He is a former executive director of the Wharton Center for Performing Arts at Michigan State University, and former vice chairman of the Michigan Council for Arts and Cultural Affairs. Beachler's leadership and inspiration—passion and commitment—were to bring serious, high-quality performing arts to central Michigan. He succeeded handsomely, under the leadership of President Clifton R. Wharton, Jr., by helping to highlight the need to construct a state-of-the-art performing arts facility on the campus of Michigan State University. Beachler, an actor, writer, and director of substantial stature in his own right, was unwavering in his goal, yet sensitive to the needs of the community. He realized the importance of building lasting relationships with the external community, for without them the popularity of the arts would wane over time. Instead, they grew in number year after year because of his ability to build important bridges with many diverse constituencies far beyond the boundaries of the campus. Beachler's influence was instrumental in keeping ticket prices reasonable so people of all income levels could experience top-quality performances.

As the actions of these individuals reflect, real leaders learn to express their passions in positive ways and to tap into the wants, hopes, and dreams of those around them. These are leaders who make indelible impressions on others, in their words and in their actions.

No Guts, No Glory

Real leadership takes guts—not the kind of guts that it takes to charge into gunfire, but the kind that makes someone stand up for his or her ideals and confront the challenges on the figurative battlefields of corporate and personal life. In the world of sports, the commonly used motivational admonition "no pain, no gain," challenges athletes to reach a goal. In the military, soldiers say "no guts, no glory." In both arenas, as in business, maintaining a safe level of achievement is seldom the best option. This ability to make tough decisions despite the threat of alienating support can be learned and taught in business and in life.

In a recession or when a company is struggling, real leadership is not necessarily having the guts to lay off half your staff, either. It's more likely to be the intestinal fortitude for instituting painful, across-the-board pay cuts in order to retain an entire workforce through rocky economic times.

That's what Paul F. Levy did at Harvard's Beth Israel Deaconess Medical Center in Boston. Though he ran into issues later in his tenure and resigned his post as CEO amid controversy in early 2011, many of the things he did as that organization's leader were admirable. At the height of the recession, Levy had the uncanny skill and the rare compassion to bring his medical and hospital staff together in a mutual sacrifice in order that fewer jobs should be cut. He had a bold vision for the medical center and dramatically enhanced its culture, reputation, and quality. Convincing doctors, nurses, and other staff to agree to pay cuts or smaller wage increases so the lowest wage earners in the hospital could keep their jobs is a remarkable feat of compassion and persuasion.

There are other gutsy leaders who understand the need for simple courage, and the willingness to stand up and make the tough decisions. These are our generations' profiles in workplace courage. A couple role models include:

- Columbia University President Lee Bollinger. He made the courageous and controversial decision to invite Iranian President Mahmoud Ahmadinejad to speak at the school's New York City campus. A First Amendment scholar, Bollinger was severely criticized for the invitation and for his own remarks that day. But in listening to the Iranian leader speak—whether one agreed with what he said or not—the world learned much more about him.

♦ Jack Welch, former head of General Electric. He is a legendary leader for many reasons. One of his gutsiest moves was to jettison several of GE's businesses, though they were highly profitable. His decision was based, in part, on the fact that these divisions had little chance of ever being the best in their respective industries. This is a courageous example of streamlining a company into greatness.

Giving Back: Leaders Who Inspire

An important aspect of a real leader's inspiration is his or her ability to recognize need in the community and respond through charity and volunteerism. This is not a uniquely American concept or the sole purview of real leaders, but true leaders unquestionably manifest and exude the humility and gratitude inherent in giving back. Where a boss's attitude may be "I've got mine; now you get yours," a real leader says, "Let me share with you what I am fortunate enough to have."

Two Americans I have long admired for their superb leadership, humanity, public service, and far-reaching contributions to countless persons and organizations are Dr. Clifton R. Wharton, Jr. and Mrs. Dolores D. Wharton. During just eight years as president and first lady of Michigan State University, the Whartons elevated the stature of the nation's first land grant university in a manner very few could. In addition to heightening the quality and breadth of the university's faculty, research programs, and community service, they also led the university's initial capital fundraising campaign, which ensured the university's success long after their tenure ended. Significantly, the Whartons' active involvement in the arts prompted the university to build a state-of-the-art performing arts facility. The Whartons recognized that all the great universities made major commitments to the arts—music, drama, dance, and painting—with corresponding facilities, faculty, and programs. In 1982, MSU bestowed the ultimate honor upon them by naming their premier arts complex the Clifton and Dolores Wharton Center for the Performing Arts.

Though much has been written about Clifton and Dolores Wharton's intellect, passion, foresight, and modesty, when you have the opportunity to speak with them it is impossible not to become caught up with how thoughtful and erudite they both are. Moreover, you're drawn closer to them through their unparalleled spontaneity, positive and upbeat demeanor, and charm. Here are two incredibly accomplished people—each a leader (Dolores Wharton has served on more than 30 corporate boards)—who continue to take an active role in each other's activities. They discovered that a genuine, enthusiastic interest in the other's work is a critical part of their individual achievements and one of the most important ingredients to a happy, successful marriage of more than 60 years.

As Dolores Wharton suggests, to lead others requires that one be knowledgeable and able to inspire. Her husband adds that leaders must be people with great integrity and honesty, and also be humane. Real leaders are "teachers" in the broadest sense. As an example, Clifton Wharton established a Presidential Fellows program at Michigan State that provides many with an opportunity to learn how to lead a university. Today, nearly a third of those who learned under his tutelage are presidents of colleges and universities.

In a diverse number of organizational settings—including leading a major university, international development, government service, and philanthropy—Wharton demonstrated time and again the virtues of listening attentively, empowering and nurturing others, developing teams, and eschewing the power trap where leaders assume they have all the answers and where arrogance unravels prior successes.

If I could follow any two individuals for a concentrated period of time to sharpen my leadership skills, Clifton and Dolores Wharton would be at the top of my list. These two pioneers, social activists, and change agents are an American treasure.

Limelight Not Required

Real leaders don't seek center stage; they seek success for others. On Thanksgiving Day 18 years ago, an Oxnard, California, father of a four-week-old boy was driving on the freeway with his wife to the San Fernando Valley. He happened to look at his son and noticed he had stopped breathing. The family quickly got off the freeway and noticed that a sporting goods store had several cars parked there so they stopped, and the mother ran into the store and yelled for help.

As fate would have it, a physician from Santa Paula had decided at the last minute to try to find a Ping-Pong table so he could play with his son, who was coming home from college. The physician was not just any physician, but Fran S. Larsen, MD, former director of the much-heralded Family Practice Residency Program at Ventura County Medical Center. Larsen ran to the couple's car and discovered that the baby had no pulse, was not breathing, and was, for all practical reasons, dead. Larsen administered CPR and chest compression, and miraculously the baby began to breathe again.

As the infant recovered and the family celebrated his renewed life, the family practitioner had silently departed. The family later uncovered the doctor's identity and had a special reunion in his medical office. They continued to bring in their son yearly so Larsen could see how he had grown. (He graduated from high school in 2011.)

A few years later, the immensely popular and highly re-garded Larsen was chosen as "Physician of the Year" for his superb medical skills, humility, community service, compassion, training of innumerable residents, successful treatment of countless patients from the region, and donating time as an team physician for one of the high schools. The world is looking for more leaders that do not seek the limelight, but simply do what they are taught to do and do it well.[7]

Sports notables Charles Woodson and Dikembe Mutombo also are giants in their respective fields. Both are media-reticent, reserved men who share a common bond: to make the world a much better place for the less fortunate, and to focus the spot-light on people in need rather than on themselves. Those are signs of a real leader.

Woodson, a former University of Michigan All-American cornerback, is the only NCAA Division I-A football player to win the prestigious Heisman Trophy as a defensive player. Today he is a standout in the National Football League, and not just for his on-the-field performance. In 2007, Woodson donated $2 million to the University of Michigan's C.S. Mott Children's Hospital and Von Voigtlander Women's Hospital. The publicity-shy Woodson earmarked his donation for pedi-atric research to help find cures for pediatric cancer, heart dis-ease, kidney disorders, and autism.

In basketball, Dikembe Mutombo is a standout on the court and off. A native of Zaire (now the Democratic Republic of the Congo) and a Georgetown University graduate, he once blocked 12 shots in a single game while he played for John Thompson's Hoyas basketball team. "Deke," as he's known to friends, went on to become one of the NBA's most prolific shot blockers in his 16-year career and earned four NBA Defensive Player of the Year awards. A leader who firmly believed in giv-ing back long before he made millions of dollars, Mutombo founded a state-of-the-art hospital and medical research facility in Kinshasa, Congo. It's a region in Africa where more than 500,000 children under the age of 5 die each year, most from preventable causes. Among other services, his hospital will train several hundred clinicians and improve treatment of HIV/AIDS patients.

Side Effect: Building Bottom Lines

Stronger leadership is an outgrowth of these individuals' inspirational giving back. By developing themselves as leaders, Woodson and Mutombo spark others around them to become real leaders, too. As you aspire to become a real leader, recognize that these torchbearers realize inspired leadership can be the fuel that helps others to achieve things they might not otherwise accomplish on their own. Real leaders also help those around them understand that upsetting the status quo is sometimes required to design a better future for their organization.

William J. Kearney, first vice president of Merrill Lynch Wealth Management, and senior resident director of its Ventura Coast office, is another extraordinary executive who leads by example. He is a mentor, community leader, and competent financial confidant who has dedicated his professional career to helping others through his work and his involvement in the Ventura County region.

For the past three decades, Kearney has been the first in the office at 4:30 a.m., works all day, then usually heads to various board meetings in the evenings. Among the types of community organizations to which Kearney lends support and expertise are higher education (including the California State University–Channel Islands), families and children through Casa Pacifica, the United Way, and the arts. Another Merrill

Lynch executive had this to say of his leader: "He's always inter-ested in finding the best answer for his clients' needs."

Inspiring leaders advance their organizations to new heights every day through their actions on and off the court, on and off the field, in the workplace, and beyond. They lead from the top, but make sure people at every level of the organization are engaged. These are leaders who also ensure that their people are heard, involved, and trained to be more innovative in mov-ing the company, the team, and their lives forward.

◆

This tradition of highlighting the history of an or-ganization can have a significant impact on leadership development. The lessons of the past, and respect and appreciation for those who came before, can instill a great sense of pride in being part of something special and unique. It also helps potential leaders understand the organization from a much deeper perspective.

When people feel that they are a part of something important or something that fills a need in the world, they take their work more personally and strive harder to see a mission fulfilled. A case in point is radio sta-tion KCLU-FM, home to the smallest yet most prolific team of professionals I have ever had the pleasure of championing. The station is an NPR affiliate owned by the Regents of California Lutheran University (CLU) in Thousand Oaks, California. Led by its indefatiga-ble and inimitable general manager Mary Olson, the four-person radio station serves Santa Barbara and Ventura counties. The station's only trained journalist is National Edward R. Murrow award-winning news director Lance Orozco. Operations and program di-rector Jim Rondeau is a substantial broadcast award-winner in his own right. The entire team is supported and complemented by the multi-talented membership director, Mia Karnatz-Shifflett.

Winner of more Mark Twain, Associated Press, Radio Television News Association, Golden Mike, Edward R. Murrow, and other awards than many of the nation's largest stations, KCLU unquestionably has a big-league news presence yet a unique and special local flavor. The station is truly the "go-to" place for live and breaking news, and the community relies on KCLU staff to keep them apprised of any natural disaster affecting Southern California.

After 17 years of broadcasting from a very cramped former student chapel in an older residence hall at CLU, KCLU moved into a new and much improved facility in 2011. Its new $3.1 million home, the Paulucci Studios, is a testament to the many years of hard work and faith from its staff and the ongoing support of its listeners, volunteers, and donors.

One of the leadership challenges I faced was convincing CLU leadership as well as many of my colleagues that a new broadcasting facility should be included on the university's list of fundraising priorities. Faced with many important academic and facility needs, this was not an easy sell. But as a university-wide capital campaign was in the planning stages, I fervently believed that raising private funds for a new freestanding broadcasting facility with state-of-the-art production studios and a "community room" (where forums of local and national topics could be discussed) would help KCLU expand its programming and reach. Moreover, KCLU could more effectively be leveraged to help raise the university's awareness, strengthen its brand, and further enhance its reputation in the region.

> After the KCLU staff made an excellent presentation to the university strategic planning committee, my colleagues rallied to approve a new station being placed on the capital campaign priority list.

◆

You Can Do It, Too

Finding your own passions and subsequent path to leadership in business and beyond requires a methodical approach punctuated by an abundance of patience and calm. We all dream of success, though everyone's dream differs. How we find our passions and accomplish our dreams depends on the effort we expend—not necessarily the money, but the work ethic. Each of us has to want it bad to achieve it. That's a part of what drives real leaders to find success. Too often in life, people— including the pseudo-leaders—"choke" under pressure because they're not passionate about what they are doing; they don't want it bad enough and are ill-prepared as a result.

To help you better recognize your own passions and develop your path to success, consider the following four-step approach:

- ◆ **Assess**. Make a comprehensive list of what you do and don't enjoy doing now; how you do and don't like to spend your time, or what does and doesn't fascinate you. As part of that, inventory your current skills and those skills you would like to learn.

- ◆ **Explore.** Ask others how they found their passions. Volunteer for a cause that interests you, take a paid or unpaid internship to learn about a business, or take a class on a topic that intrigues you.

- **Experiment.** Take a risk by doing something new or outside your comfort zone. Seek out opportunities that offer new challenges.

- **Measure.** Evaluate what you did, and how proficient you were at it. Would you benefit from more training, effort, or preparation? Was the experience invigorating? Most people can improve their skills in weaker areas even if they don't master every technique.

As I remind my students, your confidence will grow as you try new activities. I once took an acting class and studied opera. To my chagrin—or as I suspected—I had absolutely no talent in these areas. But, the experiences taught me to appreciate both arts and the skills possessed by performers. It is okay and healthy to feel strange or awkward when you're outside of your element and as you try new things. Don't be stymied by stereotypes or typecasting, either. We are all different; each of us has our own unique qualities, curiosities, and passions, and they will probably change through time.

Takeaway

- Real leaders believe in themselves, their ideals, and their goals and aspirations. If they fall down, they get back up, and try and try again until they are successful.

- Real leaders are resourceful; they know what questions to ask and of whom.

- Real leaders have passion about what they do and how they do it, enabling them to tap into the needs, hopes, and dreams of those around them. These are leaders who make indelible impressions on others, in their words and in their actions.

- Real leaders have the guts to stand up for their ideals and directly confront the challenges on the figurative battlefields of corporate and personal life. Playing it safe is seldom the best option—in business, on battlefields, or in sports.

- Real leaders inspire by giving back to the community and sharing with others. Whereas a boss's attitude is "I've got mine; now you get yours," a real leader's attitude is "Let me share with you what I am fortunate to have."

- Inspired leadership can be the fuel that helps others achieve things they might not otherwise accomplish on their own.

Real Leaders Value and Support Those They Lead

At the end of the day, you bet on people, not on strategies.

—Larry Bossidy, former CEO, Honeywell International; former chairman and CEO, Allied Signal Corporation; and former COO, General Electric Company

The current global recession has created a tsunami of workplace turmoil that has taken its toll on organizations and their employees professionally and personally. Many so-called leaders see tough times as license to use and abuse employees. Not only are discontent, distrust, and desertion running rampant in the workplace, but employees and executives are constantly worried about layoffs, trust in company leadership has waned, and job security with big corporations is nonexistent across the board. More workers are becoming small-businesspeople and setting out on their own—not by choice, but out of necessity.

This disaster scenario doesn't have to become commonplace, however. Real leaders who take charge can have a positive influence, even in tough times. These individuals recognize the true value of their greatest asset—the employee—and inspire and guide their people to succeed. A real leader's engagement and motivation bring value to employees, who, through that motivation and sense of purpose, bring value to the organization.

A Time for Leadership

Real leadership lessens workplace stress and promotes enthusiasm, loyalty, productivity, and the bottom line for everyone. It is the ripple effect compounded. This is true especially in tough economic times, because real leaders see those times as prime opportunities to step out ahead of the pack and set an example worth following.

Though real leadership makes a real difference in business performance at any time, studies show that with the right leadership, the kind that promotes engaged and enthusiastic workforces, the bottom line can go up in tough times. Research from a recent Hay Group Insight study supports that premise. The study found that employees who were engaged and enthusiastic could channel that motivation to deliver results, and employee job satisfaction improves, too.[1]

"Our research shows that even during the [economic] downturn, companies that have focused on maintaining open and honest communication with employees, ensuring that strategic directions are clear, and fostering trust and confidence in senior leaders are seeing positive returns on their investments,"[2] said William Werhane, Insights' global managing director. "Even while cutting costs, our research shows companies can still engage their employees through soft-dollar investments made by their leaders and managers." The study goes on to report:

> Companies that engage and enable their employees outperform on both revenue growth and profitability. Organizations in the top quartile on engagement demonstrate revenue growth 2.5 times that of organizations

in the bottom quartile. And, companies in the top quartile on both engagement and enablement achieve revenue growth 4.5 times greater. Moreover, companies in the top quartile on both engagement and enablement exceed industry averages on five-year return on assets, return on investment, and return on equity by 40 to 60 percent.[3]

Still not convinced that the right leader with this "touchy-feely" approach makes a difference? More statistics from the Hay study include:

- ◆ Businesses with high employee engagement levels have customer satisfaction scores 22 percent higher than companies with lower levels of employee engagement. Companies that both engage and enable employees show a 54 percent increase in customer satisfaction.

- ◆ Companies with high levels of employee engagement have 40 percent lower turnover rates than those with lower levels, and companies that both engage and enable employees show a 54 percent lower rate of voluntary turnover.[4]

Yet another survey—a seven-year study conducted by the Workplace Research Foundation and the University of Michigan—found a direct correlation between employee motivation and the financial performance of their companies. The study, "The National Benchmark Study: Employee Motivation Affects Subsequent Stock Price," involved nearly 3,500 employees at more the 840 companies in the United States. The study found that the greater employees' engagement and motivation, the better employee and company performance.[5]

Employees want to work for leaders who are upbeat, ethical, positive, industrious, energetic, fair, honest, supportive, competitive, engaged, competent, and down-to-earth. A real leader has those qualities and something more: the ability to impart those qualities to others. A real leader takes a personal interest in others' career development by mentoring and teaching instead of ordering and demanding.

The Value of Inspiration

Too many people today lack the inspiration to achieve the potential greatness within them. Real leaders provide that inspiration, and the greatness they bring out in others can be measured in achievement, satisfaction, and successes—financial and otherwise.

Abbott Laboratories is an excellent example of a 123-year-old perennial corporate leader whose enlightened and inspired vision has historically come from its top ranks and trickled down. Its leaders' beliefs and passions permeate the workplace. I was fortunate to have been a PhRMA fellow there. Abbott, a perpetual standard on "best places to work" lists, is a pharmaceutical giant. For many years, its leadership team created a great learning environment, because it prided itself on getting the best and the brightest young staff through its entry-level professional development program. The company attracts great scientists through good salaries and benefits packages as well as enlightened management practices. Young people have the opportunity to interact with many divisions within the company, working mothers have a supportive environment, and the company maintains its commitment to social responsibility. Abbott Laboratories recently decided to split into two companies to increase shareholder value, one for medical devices and the other for its research-focused drug products. Like many of America's major pharmaceutical houses confronted with healthcare reform, Abbott faces many new challenges ahead.

Remember Allan Smith from the University of Michigan in Chapter 3? He was a distinguished faculty member and dean at

Michigan's prestigious law school, and served as interim president of the university for some time. But he was neither elitist nor stuffy, and never pretentious. His career included being vice president for academic affairs at Michigan, a position that wielded considerable budgetary clout, and yet he always championed the faculty member who had a new idea. Smith is the kind of leader that inspires others to greatness.

Senator Richard Lugar does not let his position and formidable resume keep him from taking the time and making the effort to pay attention, listen, and share his wisdom and knowledge—not just with his peers and the president of the United States. He has been known to spend lunch hours jogging around the Capitol with his congressional interns, pointing out historical sites and explaining the different monuments and memorials. He also makes sure his interns sit in on important Senate committee meetings so that they are well informed and know what's going on. It is that kind of caring that inspires long-term respect and relationships with staff. It is a major reason young people gravitate to him and learn so much from him.

Fostering the Corporate Culture

Someone with a boss mindset may think corporate culture means instituting "casual Friday" in the workplace. But a leader knows that culture goes much deeper than a slogan. Perhaps the most crucial link that connects great leaders and their all-important vision is the personal value system they live, demonstrate, and teach to others. Those values become ingrained in the fabric of the business and in large part foster the corporate culture.

A culture is made up of values, perhaps those of the company's founder or a recent CEO. If either had or has a very strong ethical framework, it's very likely the company will operate in the same way. If the CEO's value system is not strong, it is quite probable the company culture will eventually model that behavior.

Most companies have mission statements or vision statements, and most have strategic plans in place, all of which affect the company's culture. Fostering a corporate culture is an intentional effort to create a desired work environment. The culture will differ, depending on the time, the place, and those involved, but each culture has a powerful influence on how business is conducted and by what kinds of people. The University of Notre Dame, for example, has a clearly defined culture based on the founding order's view of how to run a Catholic institution of higher education.

A good corporate culture unites people around core purposes, creating unity, clarity, and, for some, greater comfort. The corporate culture functions in its given industry, but it also must be effective in its marketplace. If a marketplace does not embrace the culture of a company, that company's product or service will not sell, and the company cannot thrive.

Great leaders recognize the links between culture, community, and sales, and realize that a strong corporate culture unites people and provides them with a sense of purpose bigger than any product or service. Real leaders treat employees as their greatest asset, investing in and motivating them. They expect high standards of employee behavior—the same standards they model and reinforce. Their values also include frugality, a desire to establish traditions that can be developed and built upon, and a resiliency to get right back up when knocked down by market forces. Corporate culture, if left alone, can deteriorate, resist change, or stagnate with the end result of unhappy, disillusioned, and discontented employees.

David Brandon is one of today's real leaders. He is director of athletics at the University of Michigan, where he previously served as a regent. He is also former chairman and CEO of Domino's Pizza. Brandon stands out as someone who surrounds himself with the best people—people with high ideals, people constantly striving for excellence, people with morals and integrity, people who won't break the rules, people who win the right way. He fosters that behavior in others by modeling it without pretension. He is not afraid to get his hands dirty and never asks more of anyone that he does of himself, and he is a people person who's always there when you need him.

Building Community

Inside a company, corporate culture and community are often intertwined. It is not a coincidence that many of the perennial "best places to work" today are in Silicon Valley, where companies such as Google, Facebook, Apple, and others have impressive corporate cultures, strong community ties, and unparalleled creativity. Their leadership fosters those strengths. As Massachusetts Institute of Technology's Timothy Sturgeon wrote in *How Silicon Valley Came to Be*, "the drive to play with novel technology has been a major driver in the area's success."[6]

Sharing Ownership of Ideas

A great way to foster community in the workplace is to allow ownership. Leaders know the importance of a shared commitment and pride in the work done, and so they do not take all the credit for successes, financial or otherwise, or for new developments or inventions. When you work as a leader with employees to solve a problem, it is often best to suggest direction, concepts, or steps in the process to help people come up with their own solution—even if you already have an answer. That effectively transfers the pride of ownership to your employees. When an idea "belongs" to someone, they are much more committed to it, and they act on it accordingly. And when you see this process work, it gives you a great feeling of satisfaction as a true leader. You may also learn something from them in the process.

During his active military service Navy Adm. William Thompson served as Chief of Information for the U.S. Navy (CHINFO). Like David Brandon, he believed strongly in the importance of surrounding himself with the best talent available. As a result, the efficiency of his Pentagon-based CHINFO that served the U.S. Navy and Marine Corps was unparalleled. Along with dramatically improving the quality, accuracy, and frequency of the Navy's communication with its forces around the globe, Adm. Thompson deserves credit for markedly improving the utility, education, training, and professionalism of Navy public affairs worldwide. It was Thompson, after all, who commissioned the design of CHINFO's logo and whose motto "Nothing But The Truth" has stood the test of both time and enormous challenge.

Thompson established excellent working relationships with the other commands at the Pentagon, too, because he recognized the importance of communication and collaboration, both so critical to the effectiveness of any mission or task. He transformed his organization by upgrading the talent and promoting a team attitude. He fostered an approach in which each participant was a team member and, as such, had a share in ownership of the outcomes. Everyone did his or her best as a result. Admiral Thompson's teams exemplified great skill, trust, strength, and accomplishment.

Giving Back to Employees

Human capital is a precious resource that cannot and should not take be taken for granted, and certainly should not be wasted. If it is, sooner or later business performance suffers. Amid the sound and fury of today's everyday workplace, some businesses and their leaders forget this human capital is the driving force behind their business success. They take for granted the community and team of employees that bring leadership visions to life.

♦

Fred Meijer, former CEO of Meijer—today located in several Midwestern states—was an extremely wealthy, powerful member of the area business community. Nonetheless, he remained humble, unassuming, and very caring and compassionate. He also was a member of the Butterworth Hospital board of trustees and often would arrive early at board meetings in order to distribute coupons for free ice cream cones to hospital employees.

♦

Rather than taking employees for granted, it is essential to recognize and give back. The need for praise and recognition is inherent in human nature. It is ingrained in us, and it is important for leaders and companies to recognize and act on that fact. An acknowledgment for a job well done or for initiating a new idea can go a long way toward motivating and positively reinforcing outstanding work, whether by an individual, team, or community.

Bill Walsh, legendary San Francisco 49ers football coach, was not revered simply because his teams won NFL championships and Super Bowls or because he was considered an innovative football genius. According to former all-pro quarterback Steve Young, Walsh could "see the future potential of another human being."[7]

Special Events

Times may be tough economically, but real leaders understand why now, especially, is the best time to reward employees. Sure, everyone would love a pay raise. But that simply may not be possible for many companies in tough economic times. However, tough times are not a license to disregard employee accomplishments. Rather, they may be the best times to give your staff a lift. Make a big deal of the fact that profits have remained steady during the recession (That *is* a big deal!) or that the company team working together nabbed an important contract.

Consider involving yourself in carefully planning a strategic special event. That does not mean simply throwing a party. It does mean that as a leader, it is your responsibility to seriously sit down and decide the goals to be accomplished with the event—honor top performers, for example, or launch a new marketing strategy, or, with the help of your team, introduce new products or services in the community. Done right—not necessarily extravagantly and employing a set agenda—a special event can strengthen a company's mission, solidify its corporate culture, and enhance pride in the organization.[8] All these factors are essential to sustainable growth. In lieu of a specific agenda, an employee appreciation dinner or lunch can be significant to let your people know that you are thinking of them and are grateful for their service.

Special events can send a positive, powerful message to employees and to the community, too.[9] The message of an outward-focused special event can:

◆ Instill a renewed sense of confidence and morale among employees, customers, board members, suppliers, investors, and the media.

◆ Enhance an organization's reputation.

- Mend "broken fences" that may have been knocked down during the past years of financial upheaval.

- Restore and reinforce core values, meaningful traditions, and desired behaviors of the corporate culture.

- Share the company's valued history, traditions, and key messages.

- Raise community consciousness and influence public perceptions of the business.

- Make a meaningful, positive statement about the company's future.

- Present a unique opportunity for the CEO and the executive leadership team to chart the direction of the business (and report on the company's long-term health).

- Provide an opportunity for employees at various levels of an organization to interact in a congenial setting.

Don't forget to encourage your own employees to volunteer for community organizations whose appeal they find compelling and whose special events can make a difference.

It is also important to recognize contributions in and by the community, and reinforce your company's brand at the same time. A brand, after all, instantly conveys a message, including an organization's reputation, standing, mission, and values. The brand also creates a reaction in people that reveals how much they trust the organization and desire its products or services. A strategically and carefully planned community appreciation event or open house will not only help to polish your brand, but will give you a good idea of your brand's standing in the community. Community perception of a brand can make or break a company's success. Special events can backfire, though, if they're not clearly thought out with specific goals in mind, and if the staff is not in place to carry them out.

Even if the special event is meant for a company's employees, the CEO may wish to invite community leaders in for a closer, more personalized look at the company and its people. Inviting a few strategically chosen community members and leaders can present an unmatched opportunity for sharing the real company culture and community, so long as this does not shift the focus of the event from its primary purpose. If employees sense the event that is supposed to honor them is really just an opportunity for the executives to look good in front of community leaders, it will backfire.

If the company is facing changes or looking to expand into new markets or offer new products, a special event can be a great way to introduce the changes in a way that fosters ownership. It helps employees feel on board for the new direction, and creates momentum for going forward.

Giving Back to the Community

Leadership, as you've read in these pages, takes many forms: formal and informal, highly visible and subtle as well. Real leaders give back to their communities in much the same multi-faceted way and, in doing so, are role models for others to follow. Leading with the example of having a positive impact on those less knowledgeable or less fortunate teaches other aspiring leaders to always be humble and compassionate in how they live their lives.

Dusty Baker is legendary and his legacy is powerful—not just in Major League Baseball. Baker is the only man in MLB to be named manager of the year three times. The current manager of the Cincinnati Reds, Baker also played 16 seasons with Atlanta, Los Angeles, San Francisco, and Oakland; went with his teams to three World Series; and won the pennant in 1981. He was named to the All-Time Los Angeles Dodgers team and as a manager named to the All-Time San Francisco Giants team. But beyond his sports leadership accolades, honors, and awards, Baker is a real leader who believes in giving back.

A prostate cancer survivor, Baker deeply believes in helping educate others about prostate cancer. He is active in fundraising efforts for prostate cancer research and treatment, too. "Sometimes you wonder what's your purpose on Earth," Baker said. "I know baseball wasn't my only purpose. Maybe I'm supposed to spread the word and help people with cancer."[10] Baker also founded the nonprofit Dusty Baker International Baseball Academy, which focuses not only on athletics but also on "the core principles of developing self-confidence, self-reliance, and self-discipline."

Reflecting his values that combine sportsmanship, scholarship, and humanity, the following Ralph Waldo Emerson quotation hangs in his office:

> To laugh often and much; to win the respect of intelligent people and the affection of children; to earn the appreciation of honest critics and endure the betrayal of false friends; to appreciate beauty, to find the best in others; to leave the world a bit better, whether by a healthy child, a garden patch or a redeemed social condition; to know even one life has breathed easier because you have lived. This is to have succeeded.[11]

Enduring Leadership

Historically, an important mark of a successful leader has been whether his or her accomplishments endure through time. Despite today's rapidly changing global economy, that measure of true success remains the same. Real leaders such as Dusty Baker make a difference in the lives of those around them and in the companies, workplaces, and communities where they work and live no matter the changing times or external forces.

Real leaders create and leave legacies for those who come after them. Those legacies can be sweeping and grand, such as Ray Kroc and the business model he developed for McDonald's that revolutionized the fast-food industry, or Jack Welch, who as the leader of General Electric rebuilt the once-struggling company into a giant powerhouse.

Or, a leadership legacy can take place on a much smaller scale, but just as powerfully for the individuals involved. The way Senator Lugar mentors interns in his Washington, D.C., Senate office is a great example. His willingness to spend time with those young people creates a lasting impression—a legacy. Not only does it help these young leaders in their personal leadership growth, but it also creates a precedent that they will likely follow in the future with their own people.

A Model for Others

I was privileged to have worked with a number of outstanding physicians during my time in the healthcare industry, including a select few whose extraordinary medical skills were exceeded only by their humanity. For nine years, I worked with Richard Schreiner, MD, in his dual role as chairman of the department of pediatrics and as physician-in-chief of Riley Hospital for Children in Indianapolis. A neonatologist by training, Schreiner transformed a good pediatrics department into a preeminent one, which continues to serve as a model for other hospitals across Indiana and the United States.

Schreiner readily admits that he had no specific management training before taking over the department of pediatrics, only a passion to provide children with the best care possible.[12] Yet, his personality and desire to succeed exemplify several attributes that today's leaders should emulate:

- ◆ Technical excellence with an unparalleled sense of modesty.

- ◆ Frugality in business, but an unbounded generosity toward his patients and their families.

- ◆ The humility and wisdom to hire and retain a highly accomplished, collegial, and caring team of medical professionals (including Drs. Jim Lemons, neonatology; Ora Pescovitz, endocrine/diabetes; Howard Eigen, pulmonary; and others, including Jay Grosfeld, a pediatric surgeon and chair of the surgery department).

- ◆ A record of supporting employees, constantly encouraging them to treat one another, very ill children, and their parents and families in the most caring way possible, while avoiding the temptation to micromanage them.

A bronze statue of Dr. Schreiner now stands in the lobby of Riley Hospital. It is fitting that Schreiner never sought such an honor. Instead, a colleague, supported by his legion of friends and associates, commissioned a teenage sculptor to create a life-sized statue of his likeness, a testament not only to one of the giants in pediatric medicine, but also to a leader who transformed the hospital and the department of pediatrics into a national center of excellence.

The Happiness Factor

Is your office or company a happy place? Seriously—if someone walked into your office or company or place of business for the first time today, what would be his or her impression? If he or she were to think that this is a happy and productive place, that's a plus. A happy workplace is a sign of tangible leadership. This cannot be overemphasized: happy workers make the best workers. Performance of a team is often determined, in part, by whether their leadership celebrates their successes and allows them to celebrate.

How would you rate your workplace on the "happiness" scale? If it scores low, what tangible things can you do to make it a happier and more productive place? Do your company and its leadership celebrate the successes of employees? If not, why not? What can you do to make a difference?

A positive company culture can help curb absenteeism, boost morale, and enhance productivity. Leaders should present a positive attitude, which includes a smile, a sense of humor, and a supportive manner when dealing with staff. Real leaders expect high standards and values among their employees, and they model and reinforce those standards of honesty, resiliency, commitment, and integrity in their own behavior. All of this contributes to the company's culture and influences how the company is led and managed. Some company cultures are stronger than others, but all influence the selection of personnel, workplace ethics, and relationships— among employees, with customers, and with the community. Some cultures are longstanding, whereas others have been formed more recently. Companies with strong corporate cultures that have contributed to long-term success include GE, Procter & Gamble, Four Seasons, Abbott, Hewlett-Packard, IBM, and BMW.

A leader doesn't have to be charismatic, tall, attractive, or wealthy to be successful, but it is important to be able to propel others to achieve success. What are the traits that help to build inspiring leaders? What can you do to acquire those skills and strengthen existing ones? In the absence of external leadership, what can you do to unlock your internal leadership passion? How can you encourage others to do the same?

You Can Do It, Too

Some concrete steps that you can take to enhance your real leadership positioning include:

- Praising others when appropriate, and constructively counseling them at other times. Remember: a leader must also be a teacher.
- Indemnifying the team concept, but not being afraid to take charge or give others the reins when appropriate.
- Championing your people and promoting them actively.
- Taking risks as appropriate. That means helping the organization and others excel by removing roadblocks and obstacles to their success.
- Sacrificing for the team.
- Being a cheerleader by continuously encouraging your staff to succeed.
- Underscoring your team's importance to the overall success of the organization by appropriately conveying their contributions.

- Regularly soliciting feedback from your team. After all, the workplace is hardly static; therefore, continuous learning and leading go hand in hand.

Takeaway

- Worker discontent and distrust in today's workplace is a direct result of leadership failures.

- Real leaders set the example and step out ahead of the competition. Leadership done right cuts down on workplace stress and promotes enthusiasm, loyalty, and productivity, and improves the company's bottom line.

- A leader's vision and values set the stage, and as the leader lives those values and conveys that vision, they become ingrained in the fabric of the organization and, in turn, help foster its corporate culture.

- Community, culture, and creativity working together in an organization fuel bottom-line success.

- Real leaders step back and allow employees to take credit for ideas and actions. Leaders know the importance of assigning the pride of ownership to others. With ownership, employees generally are more committed to an idea or activity. It's a leader's job to suggest direction, ideas, and even guide the process to help employees come up with solutions.

- Real leaders don't play favorites among their staff. Instead, they consciously create a more level playing field for their staff so that all ideas are evaluated on their merits and objective job appraisal trumps cronyism.

- Leadership legacies take on many forms— from the small, thoughtful acts to major, marketplace-shifting strategies. What is universal, however, is that a real leader leaves his or her legacy as a model of behavior for those who follow.

- Tough times are not a license to squeeze employees or to ignore their accomplishments. In rough economic times, it's more important than ever to recognize that your employees are willing to work harder, not only to maintain the status quo, but also to propel the company forward. Leaders should honor and celebrate their employees.

- Real leaders know when it's time to move on or out: they leave "at the top of their game" unlike houseguests who overstay their welcome.

Chapter 6

Real Leaders Know When to Shut Up and Get Out of the Way

The best executive is the one who has sense enough to pick good men to do what he wants done and self-restraint to keep from meddling with them while they do it.

—Theodore Roosevelt

Real leaders are not egomaniacs who constantly demand center stage, take all the credit, and expect the kudos. Instead, they know when to step aside and watch others be recognized for the success they have achieved. They are willing to allow others to achieve success, and their own success follows. A goal real leaders set for themselves is to build a pervasive culture of "leaders for tomorrow" in their organizations. One of my favorite iterations is, "It is amazing how much can be accomplished if no one cares who gets the credit."

In Chapter 1, you read President Obama's thoughts on leadership and the importance of setting the stage, then stepping aside. Real leaders set the stage, and know when to allow those they lead to step to the front. They know how and when to get out of the way. This important leadership practice helps infuse a greater sense of shared ownership and growth in workers and enables the organization to be much more responsive to market challenges. Complacency is replaced with dispatch, autocratic behavior is exchanged for entrepreneurialism, and convention is supplanted by innovation. The result is an organization that is better positioned to react quickly and stay well ahead of the competition, while team members take joy in their work, boosting bottom lines in the process.

Stepping Aside

Allan Smith at the University of Michigan is a brilliant example of a leader who lays the foundation and then moves out of the way to watch his organization's successes mount. Smith enhanced and improved on the university's decentralized system of operations by delegating substantial autonomy to the deans of the schools and colleges, as well as to the directors of the research institutes. That approach, still in effect today, helped foster ownership among all units of the university. As I mentioned in the last chapter, ownership tends to promote better, more productive performance.

That's not the norm, however, in major corporations, public or private. Typically, leaders assume command, then take their place front and center and above everyone. They are positioned to take the glory or the fall, depending on the success or failure of an operation. But as often happens, should a problem occur, instead of taking the fall, the bosses out in front point their fingers at someone else, which further compounds disappointment and disillusionment among employees and staff. Front and center is *not* always the best location if a leader hopes to get the most from employees and others who follow.

The best position for a real leader—the role that has the greatest chance of success—is as the facilitator. This means you as a real leader train, teach, support, and guide others, then move out of the way to allow them to succeed. The leader's real job is to prepare his or her troops for the task or goal and then stand back to allow those troops—employees or whomever—to do their jobs, accomplish the defined goals, *and* take the credit (or, at the least, move forward with them arm in arm). To further ensure success, a leader knows how to rally his or her troops so that they will understand and support the plan of action, participate in the vision, and respect the process. Followers must understand the leader's vision, values, character, and beliefs; they must have faith in their leader's commitment and the achievability of his or her goals.

Change Agents

Few people like change; it is especially difficult to implement changes in a large organization. But as a leader, you can get the wheels of change moving with your courage, resolve, patience, and interpersonal skills. Real leaders understand the importance of initiating changes that will be lasting. They know how to fully and properly prepare employees and staff for change, and how and when to step aside so employees can embrace and take ownership of it. A leader does all this while maintaining a leadership role.

For real and aspiring leaders, the first step in the process is to recognize the importance of preparing your team for changes that lie ahead. Then with the right tools and training, your team—and you—will succeed. Often companies without real leadership today fail to see beyond the near term and aren't willing to invest the time or money on the front end in preparation and training, and consequently lose out on the back end and bottom line. Employees often end up disgruntled, unhappy, and unproductive, because they haven't been given the proper preparation or environment in which they could do their jobs. Despite today's economy and tight job market, some discontented employees may even quit, leaving a company with the headache, hassle, and cost of having to replace them.

◆

"You never change things by fighting the existing reality. To change something, build a new model that makes the existing model obsolete."[1]

—R. Buckminster Fuller

◆

Retired Adm. Thompson is an exceptional facilitator who is able to smoothly effect change. He has infectious enthusiasm about whatever he does. He is modest, kind, and humble, yet also determined, deceptively sharp, well-connected, and highly respected for his professionalism, ethics, and knowledge. Both in his military career and after his retirement as president of the U.S. Navy Memorial, Adm. Thompson exemplified the role of a real leader.

Thompson facilitates success with an all-encompassing approach: he outlines his goals, obtains the backing of his superiors to help support those goals, and then organizes a team of experts to study, analyze, and suggest ways to accomplish the goals. By enlisting others in the process, he helps remove any barriers to implementing changes. Thompson will lay the foundation, which includes making sure roles and responsibilities of each team member are clearly defined, then he adopts a low profile. He steps out of the way so he doesn't interfere with the process that's been established. He lets his team members do what they were trained to do to accomplish the clearly defined goals. His team members know, though, that if they need counsel, a sounding board, or something more, Thompson is always there.

Two other superb leaders I have worked with are Navy Captains Ron Wildermuth and Jim Mitchell. I worked around the clock with the very accomplished Wildermuth during the late 1980s when the Navy hit radar sites in Libya. During the early 1990s, I supported NATO operations related to the Bosnian War under the very skillful guidance of Navy Captain Jim Mitchell. Wildermuth and Mitchell were savvy, skilled, industrious, and excellent teachers.

Another real leader who facilitated success with his actions and approach is Adm. William J. Crowe, Jr., who, among other appointments, served as Chairman of the Joint Chiefs of Staff in 1989 while I was on annual active duty in their Public Affairs Office. The office consisted of a team of public information officers, enlisted personnel, and civilians charged with serving multiple commands worldwide. The team members were required to have broad knowledge of current operations and events, great flexibility, and lightning-fast reaction time. The job also required a well-oiled operations machine that could do an incredible job no matter the task. The information team's superior efficiency was not solely due to the fact that it was a military operation. It was because of the leadership ripple effect: Crowe, one of the very few commanders I ever met who had a PhD, set the tone and the stage for the team to assist and support commanding officers across the globe on a moment's notice. The team members enjoyed doing the job and doing it well. The team was respected, appreciated, and treated well, and, in turn, did the best possible job. Not surprisingly, attrition on that team was low.

The Momentum Phenomenon

Enthusiasm is contagious. Real leaders use that to their and their company's advantage. Both Thompson and Crowe not only had the right idea about how to manage a team, but their enthusiasm toward their goals was infectious, with top-notch work as the result. Their team members wanted to do the best job possible because that's what their leader expected of them.

From a business perspective, that kind of enthusiasm provides nearly unstoppable momentum that propels employees and others to levels of achievement well beyond set goals. Those goals can be small and personal, or seemingly overwhelming with far-reaching effects. Whichever the case, real leadership can mean the difference between great success and great failure in accomplishing any goals.

Remember Beth Israel Deaconess Medical Center's Paul Levy, mentioned in Chapter 4? The medical center was facing major layoffs during the current recession. Levy persuaded the entire staff to accept pay adjustments so that lower-paid employees could keep their jobs. As a real leader—one with inherent abilities of persuasion—Levy set a monumental goal, believed in the goal, worked with others to understand the importance of the goal, generated momentum to move forward toward the goal, and eventually achieved it.

No matter the scale of the goal or the degree of change required, it all starts with real leadership. After preparing their team, real leaders then work toward achieving their goals one step at a time, building on each successful accomplishment of those they lead.

Adversity as a Motivator

Reading all the leadership books in the world doesn't automatically make someone a real leader. Knowing how to lead takes experience and experimentation with different solutions for different situations. After all, no two situations in the workplace will ever be exactly the same, and rapidly increasing changes in the world will ensure that this will continue.

Adversity and failure, too, provide some of the best experiences and the greatest lessons in life. The key, though, is to look at life's adverse lessons with a positive spin, and approach them with patience rather than panic. Then, you emerge from difficult circumstances with more success and poise, and learn the important lessons of leadership in the process.

Academy Award winner for Best Picture, *The King's Speech* tells the story of a leader faced with a tremendous crisis of conviction. Trying to overcome a lifelong speech impediment and a timid spirit to answer the call of leadership at the outset of World War II, King George VI of England had to learn trust in others, admit and face his weakness, and persevere to reach a goal.

This kind of adversity can be a great motivator. If, at a job interview, you have ever been asked "What is the biggest failure or the biggest challenge you've ever experienced?" you have no doubt been faced with the dilemma of exposing a weakness at the time when you most want to promote your strengths. The truth is that many people are at their best and do their best work when everything else appears to be at its worst. The lessons of history have taught us that leaders and people in general often emerge from adversity better and more accomplished. How an individual deals with and emerges from serious challenges, adverse circumstances, or failures can often provide an insight into his or her individual capabilities and true persona.

Moreover, among the most fundamental tasks of a leader is to prepare the organization for a crisis, and then be able to function effectively when a crisis occurs. In his book *Managing the Non-Profit Organization*, Peter F. Drucker writes:

> The most important task of an organization's leader is to anticipate crisis. Perhaps not to avert it, but to anticipate it. To wait until the crisis hits is already abdication. One has to make the organization capable of anticipating the storm, weathering it, and in fact, being ahead of it. That is called innovation, constant renewal. You cannot prevent a major catastrophe, but you can build an organization that is battle-ready, that has high morale, and also has been through a crisis, knows how to behave, trusts itself, and where people can trust one another.[2]

Rebounding With Strength

Rebounding from adversity is a skill that cannot be taught. An individual has to experience adversity firsthand, and struggle out of it, to understand what it is and to comprehend its value for success in life. Some of the greatest business leaders on record are people who faced tremendous adversity and emerged stronger, wiser, and with more passion and determination to succeed. These losers-turned-winners, with their indefatigable spirits, are able to nurture complete trust among their staff and, because of this, have an innate ability to inspire a workforce to reach new heights and do their best work.

◆

"Smooth seas do not make skillful sailors."
—African proverb

◆

Credentials, a top-notch education, a strong upbringing—even impeccable values—also aren't enough to make a great leader. Instead, it takes the added experience of enduring hardship—even failure—and persevering to learn the secrets for knowing what to do in any situation. A few real leaders I know of who have triumphed over adversities include:

- ◆ Paul Orfalea, whom I brought to the Corporate Leaders Breakfast speaker series I started. The founder of Kinko's, he discusses his condition in his book, *Copy This: Lessons from a Hyperactive Dyslexic Who Turned a Bright Idea into One of America's Best Companies* (Workman Publishing, 2005).

- ◆ Bill Walsh, legendary coach and general manager of the San Francisco 49ers. He was blackballed by Cleveland Bengals' coach Paul Brown in a move that nearly ended his NFL career.

- U.S. Sen. John McCain. His Navy plane was shot down during the Vietnam War, then he was imprisoned and tortured in the notorious "Hanoi Hilton" in North Vietnam.

- Hank Greenberg, baseball Hall of Famer. He performed magnificently despite constant anti-Semitic verbal abuse and death threats.

- Frank Gehry, well-known and much-lauded architect. He had to overcome strong anti-Semitism early in his life.

- Actress Marlee Matlin, a profoundly deaf but skilled and talented actress. She took the Oscar for Best Actress in 1986.

- Muhammad Ali, three-time heavyweight champion of the world. He was confronted by racial hatred early in life.

- U.S. Sen. Daniel Inouye, a Japanese-American and World War II hero. He lost his hand when he was severely wounded in combat.

- C. Paige Vickery, a highly successful classical musician, conductor, and educator and now a diplomat who overcame Tourette's syndrome.

- Drew Barrymore, actress. She overcame a troubled childhood and resurrected her career.

Building Tomorrow's Leaders

Across the globe, international leaders struggle with a multitude of crises—from economic and political to environmental and social. In the United States, partisanship and rancor seem to trump compromise and consensus from Sacramento, California, to Washington, D.C. Unfortunately, the absence of effective leadership is not limited to the halls of state legislatures or Congress, but also plagues both Wall Street and the C-suites of the nation's companies. Where are the real leaders who can effectively guide us through the crises that we face? Government and business must develop many more leaders with the expertise to balance long-term strategy with a predisposition to tackle urgent problems and teach as they go.

Today's businesses and institutions must make a conscious commitment to teach managers as well as lower-level employees how to become leaders. Presidents, CEOs, and members of the executive team who take the time to teach, mentor, and guide their lieutenants and associates are more successful in driving performance. Staff retention is also higher, and that cuts costs, too. Additionally, developing young talent ensures that the company has an easy transition when it comes time for a leader to step aside.

The military often provides an excellent training ground for honing leadership skills that can be used throughout life and work experiences. For example, whether you're at sea or a member of a squadron or a platoon, working in a closed environment forces you and your team to solve problems quickly and successfully, because lives are often at stake. If team members are empowered, if they understand the importance of taking the lead to resolve issues, if they recognize clarity of purpose, and if they believe in their abilities, they are much more likely to be successful. All this contributes to nurturing leadership skills.

Start Early

Our two sons were born in Ann Arbor, Michigan, at the University of Michigan Hospital. They both had mastered the famous fight song "Hail to the Victors" before they were in kindergarten. One of the numerous benefits of growing up in a university community is that renowned scholars, leaders, and families from all over the world surround you. The richness of diversity in Ann Arbor cannot be overstated.

We were fortunate that our two sons had some of the most knowledgeable, caring, and committed coaches during the 14 years we lived in Ann Arbor and later in Indianapolis, where our sons graduated from Park Tudor High School. Tom Huntzicker, Larry Darling, Tom Page, and Scott Fischer were some of the coaches we remember fondly, for they were real leaders. These men applied discipline with genuine care and concern for the students' welfare. They taught youngsters how to play for the love of the game, no matter what sport they happened to be playing at the time. They also taught them how to behave on and off the field, court, or ice with class, dignity, and respect for all. And, they all emphasized the importance of doing well academically.

The GE Difference

There's a reason why leader extraordinaire John F. "Jack" Welch (of General Electric fame) and his successor, Jeff Immelt, are often mentioned in books on leadership, management, and training. They both believe strongly in grooming tomorrow's leaders as a part of their personal leadership responsibility. In fact, Welch groomed Immelt, his successor at GE's helm.

For decades, General Electric has been committed to training its future leaders through GE Crotonville, now known as the John F. Welch Leadership Development Center. Based in Ossining, New York, today it is an international leadership training organization that every year hosts thousands of employees from GE's operations worldwide. Among its offerings for future leaders are:

- ◆ Executive courses in leadership, innovation, strategy, and manager development.

- Leadership courses for new managers focusing on development, business impact, and external focus.
- Essential skills courses, such as hiring, presentations, team building, and project management.
- Customer programs including executive briefings, change management, and integration.[3]

As a testament to the program's success, 90 percent of GE's top 600 leaders have been promoted from within the company. They have to be doing something right!

Go Inside!

Many corporations mistakenly act as if building leadership means hiring talent from top-shelf consulting companies or hiring up-and-comers from the best academic institutions. Both are strategies that sap financial resources in tough and not-so-tough economic times; more important, neither strategy fills the bill.

Several years ago, I had just joined a large corporation and had aspirations of climbing the corporate ladder. As an enthusiastic new hire, I wanted to make the most of the opportunities the company offered. So I asked my boss what programs the company had to identify and develop future leaders from within the company. My obviously surprised and confused boss responded by saying that the company's current practice was to recruit talent from the outside. To spend institutional resources on leadership development, he said, would create unrest in the C-suite, lead to controversy because there would be "winners and losers," and amount to showing preferential treatment in an otherwise-egalitarian environment. I didn't stay at that company very long. Any business, large or small, that prefers to recruit from the outside rather than groom and promote from within—intra-organizational leadership development—dooms itself to failure over the long haul.

Leadership learning shouldn't be confined only to upper echelons of corporations, either. Companies and their executives must develop an organizational culture that builds future leaders from the ground up, that teaches not only leadership skills, but also an understanding of business strategy and culture. That approach helps deliver lasting results and true innovation. The core of a diverse organization, after all, should be internally developed leaders who understand the business strategy and culture, and who have the staff and network to speed the delivery of work and the internal credibility to drive insightful change.

"The degree to which firms (small, medium and large) work on leadership development within an organization typically is directly correlated to an organization's continuity of strong leadership and management," says Limoneira's Harold Edwards.[4] Managing this discipline from the top down is a critical job of the CEO. Edwards offers a few thoughts on his approach to intra-organizational leadership development:

> In any size organization, I feel it is important to embrace a process of defining critical leadership competencies for each managerial role within an organization. It is then important to identify and evaluate the actual competencies displayed by each manager within an organization and to compare them to the defined leadership competencies for each managerial role. This process will create a "gap analysis" that will identify areas of competency and leadership development requirements critical for tomorrow's leaders to display. Once these gaps are identified, it is easier to create leadership development programs that strengthen and enhance the competencies in which managers need to improve.[5]

The Power of Empowerment

Leadership in the 21st century is about leading at all levels, and not simply restricting it to job title, agrees Rick Lash, director of the Hay Group's Leadership and Talent Practice and co-leader of the Best Companies for Leadership Study. Among the Top 20 companies for leadership, 100 percent provide employees at every level of their organization the opportunity to develop the capabilities needed to lead others, according to their study released in early 2011. "Ninety percent of the Top 20 companies report that people are expected to lead regardless of whether they have a formal position of authority," the study reports.[6]

Companies like the Hay Group's Top 20 empower their employees. *Empower* is a popular buzzword these days, and I have heard it grossly misused. The word literally means to give power or authority. But it implies many conditions that are often missed: How should power be transferred to individuals who are ready to take on the tasks and responsibilities of leadership? How are individuals made to feel that they are ready for this challenge? Empowerment should embody a serious approach to helping individuals gain experience, knowledge, and insight so they can successfully handle issues and problems on their own.

Don't be afraid to transfer pride of authorship, says Traverse City businessman Mark VanderKlipp, who has learned that essential lesson from many mentors in similar positions of authority. Along with his management team, VanderKlipp has achieved perhaps the most difficult aspect of managing a business—a transition in ownership from the founding group to a second generation—when he led the internal process of transition during an eight-year period that resulted in a structurally and financially successful shift to new ownership, something the firm's competitors are still grappling with. His next challenge will be selecting the third generation of firm leaders and mentoring them to take over someday. That process has already begun.[7]

◆

"It seems to me it's up to the leader to set the goal but then to include as broad a group of people as possible in the decision-making about how do we get from where we are to achieve that goal, and that kind of an inclusive decision-making process, I think, ensures that change is actually lasting because those who are left behind after the leader departs have embraced it and it's their change."[8]

—Former U.S. Defense Secretary Robert M. Gates

◆

Growing as a Leader

Whether a leader has won his or her "bars" on the battlefield, in the boardroom, or beyond, teaching and learning are life-long. Those who mentor and teach new leaders grow as leaders themselves. Larry Ames is one of those special leaders who have helped others develop. The now-retired sports editor of the *Ventura County Star* recounts his role in the formation of one such leader:

As assistant sports editor/schools at the *Boston Globe* from 1979-1994, one of my responsibilities was to hire, train, and supervise our college interns from colleges from across Greater Boston.... One year, as I was starting a hiring period, I received a phone call from B.J. Schecter, a freshman at Northeastern University in Boston. He said he was applying for one of the co-op positions in the sports department, and that I was going to hire him. I told Schecter that we normally didn't hire freshmen, because we wanted them to become acclimated to college academic life before we would consider them. But I was fascinated by my conversation with Schecter and decided to hire him.

I was greatly rewarded by my decision. B.J. worked harder than anyone I had ever hired, and he listened and learned better, too. When B.J. graduated from college *Sports Illustrated* hired him as a researcher/reporter. B.J.'s hard work and determination has never waned. Today, he is executive editor of SI.com, the magazine's highly successful Website.

I never tried to figure out if Schecter was a born leader or someone who learned to lead. I do know that hiring him made me a better leader, and was an experiment which helped my leadership role and created several new leaders.[9]

Building a Leadership Pipeline

Today's workplace suffers no shortage of "leaders-in-waiting," young talent hoping to be identified, mentored, challenged, and developed by senior leadership. The shortage, instead, is in companies willing to make the commitment to leadership mentoring. Too few organizations recognize the competitive edge that can result from building this conduit or pipeline of future leaders. Real leaders recognize that the greater the number of quality ideas that emerge across various levels of a business, the greater the likelihood that better decisions will be made. The flattening of corporate leadership—in which leadership is spread across the organization and throughout all levels rather than concentrated in the hands of a few at the top—is occurring in today's top leadership companies, as reflected in the Hay Group study mentioned previously. To accomplish that, however, takes leadership training, and those companies that commit to it are the most successful.

Pipeline Models

The spectacular rise of the University of Southern California as an academic powerhouse during the past two decades is a prime example of what can happen with the right infrastructure—or leadership pipeline—in place. Rather than tap talent from top academic institutions, well-known military brass, or stalwart corporate giants such as GE, Boeing, IBM, Four Seasons, or Ritz-Carlton, the school's leadership opted to build future leaders internally, from the ground up. That way up-and-coming leaders would already understand the business—USC—and its strategy and culture.

Today's businesses, large and small, could do well by modeling their leadership pipeline after that of the U.S. military, specifically the U.S. Marines. Of course, bellowing drill sergeants, long runs in double time, and tactical weapons practice would not be on the agenda in future business leadership training. But strategic thinking, learning by doing, executing complex plans, figurative tactical weapons use, and so on, are lessons from the military that can be useful. Junior officers learn to be strategic thinkers, to develop and execute complex plans, to supervise and motivate enlisted personnel, to be accountable for expensive equipment, and to be calm under intense pressure. Learning by doing is also a critical aspect of training, as are regular counseling, critiquing, challenging, and correcting of performance by senior leaders. If the goals are to have employees who know the competition and the playing field, understand the objectives, are well-trained to achieve those objectives, and can accomplish them quickly and efficiently, then the Marines provide an excellent example of how to achieve them.

Step-by-Step Training

The right kind of built-in, orchestrated leadership training—the right leadership pipeline—is one way a company can differentiate itself from the competition and thus attract top talent. Consider the following sound approaches in developing your leaders for tomorrow. Try them, and your company will likely be more successful:

- **Develop bench strength.** Success in sports, as in business, requires a team of starters and those on the bench who can be called upon at critical times. This depth of talent wins championships and captures new business.

- **Develop leaders at every level of the organization.** Most organizations are complex and require talent development across the company. A reservoir of emerging leaders sustains an organization's culture and brand.

- **Develop numerous ways that younger talent can have increasing responsibilities.** Executives and other leaders should be required to spend quality time identifying and developing talent deep within the organization. Top executives are more successful, too, if they regularly provide learning opportunities for young managers.

- **Develop the human resources function.** Its responsibilities should include oversight of an in-house leadership development curriculum, which is essential to provide added value to the organization. A unified, systematic leadership development approach is far more effective than unrelated, episodic efforts by various departments.

- **Develop the moral fiber, values, and ethical standards that often are lacking in today's leaders.** When aspiring leaders are given real-world challenges that involve right and wrong, they learn lasting lessons. Core values and ethical principles are more quickly ingrained when learned early in a career.

When the Pipeline Runs Smoothly

Selection of personnel and leadership development are two of the most important responsibilities of an executive. In my nine years as head of marketing, public relations, physician outreach, and hospital affiliations at Indiana University Medical Center, I had the best team of professionals one could assemble for healthcare. At that time, IU Medical Center consisted of Riley Hospital for Children, Indiana University School of Medicine, and Indiana University Hospital. Our function was called Medical Center Relations, and it consisted of the following subdivisions: physician and consumer referral systems; publications; media relations; outreach to practicing physicians across Indiana and beyond; hospital affiliations; speakers bureau; and marketing, including a substantial commitment to market research, wayfinding, and other tasks.

As I reflect back on those turbulent years of hospital alignment, merger frenzy, and cost containment, I remember superb leaders—members of my team, including Mary Minix, Kathryn Alexander, Lynaire White, Jan Michelson, Karen Alter, Kathleen Hopper, Brian Kelley, Suzie Mathis, Kim Harper, Barbara McElroy, Barbara Hollingsworth, and others. Their leadership was characterized by being very approachable, excellent listeners and writers, gifted researchers, and able to develop deep trust with the community as well as academic physicians and hospital staffs. Their communication styles were open, consultative, clear, and persuasive. Each had a stellar work ethic and believed that passion was fundamental to their success, because if you do not put your heart into your work, you will not succeed. They loved their work and they had very high standards. I've never worked with a more dedicated group of outstanding professionals. Most important, though, each was highly ethical and fully dedicated to our mission, which was to help all who had a connection with our medical centers, be it the very sick child in Riley or adult patient in University Hospital and the medical and health professionals attending to them, the referring physician who needed to be connected quickly with the attending faculty physician, the hospital executive in an outlying Indiana hospital who needed assistance, the consumer trying to navigate the complexities of the healthcare environment, or the businessperson in need of a speaker.

◆

Alden B. Dow, noted architect and son of Dow Chemical Company founder Herbert Dow, once said that "an artist in pursuit of his profession should exhibit a balance of honesty, humility, and enthusiasm. Honesty, more than sincerity; humility, the ability to give and take gracefully; and enthusiasm, the ardent pursuit of expression." Dow's employees often referred to this statement as "HH&E."[10]

◆

Regional Leadership Programs

Beyond colleges and universities, leadership training is not the sole purview or responsibility of corporations and businesses. Many community and business organizations, as well as regional groups, colleges, and universities, offer insightful and valuable leadership education experiences. Some of the programs best positioned to identify and develop future leaders often are associated with local chambers of commerce. I have participated in several of these myself, including Leadership San Francisco, and Stanley K. Lacy's Executive Leadership Program Opportunity Indianapolis.

Areas of Study

The issues and topics of these kinds of leadership programs vary depending on the level of sophistication and economic health of the specific community or region. Nonetheless, the programs generally share important leadership development goals, including:

- Becoming better informed about pressing community issues and needs.
- Getting to know business and civic leaders who have been instrumental in shaping the community.
- Acquiring the knowledge and resources to become effective change agents in the community.
- Determining each class member's specific passion, connecting with others, and broadening horizons.
- Building an extended network of community contacts, friends, and mentors.
- Developing more volunteer and board participation in not-for-profit organizations in the area.

Most programs typically run from eight to 11 months. Each new class will usually spend a day learning about the community from accomplished leaders. They will also learn about pertinent challenges facing the community, focus on each class member's personal leadership skills, and explore growth opportunities. Many programs begin with a retreat of some sort (often a two-day event) that can include:

- Leadership training exercises.
- Lectures by leadership trailblazers.
- Exploration of personal leadership styles.
- Discussions and discoveries related to diversity in people and perspectives.
- Interactive learning among class members.

Added Advantages of Training

Employers as well as employees can reap major benefits from these leadership programs. Program graduates—as knowledgeable future leaders—are more valuable to their companies. A company's leadership pipeline is enriched, and program graduates are more effective mentors for their coworkers. As an added bonus, the company's brand gets a boost through its employees' participation with other highly regarded companies, especially if a company sponsors programs or events as part of the leadership training.

More businesses and industry leaders should consider getting involved in chamber-endorsed leadership programs across the country. These programs are vital to communities and operate with your company's interest in mind: to create real leaders for the future of your company and community.

Leaders in Oft-Overlooked Places

Potential leaders can be anywhere, including the often-overlooked arena of the arts. When work, commitment, and pleasure combine to create passion, nothing is impossible. Music, fine arts, and theater demand an above-average level of creativity as well as discipline, commitment, and passion—all valuable traits often lacking in today's struggling businesses.

William Revelli at the University of Michigan married his love of music with the highest standards of excellence and an uncanny ability to inspire college students with unremitting discipline. Under Revelli's direction, the Michigan marching band was innovative—the first to use original scores for their band's shows, and employ synchronized music and movements. They were highly praised for their precision, formations, and style. Revelli was tough on his young band members and would not accept mediocrity. His exceptionally high standards demanded strong commitment from his team members—not only to their music, but also in their lives. The university's reputation as a premiere music institution is due, in large part, to Revelli's influence. He would have made an excellent corporate leader.

He is a great leader from the arts, but great leadership can come from anywhere: on the field, court, or track, or from the humblest community college in your area. There are people around you who might do seemingly ordinary things, and suddenly a movement is started. Consider Rosa Parks, a young African-American civil rights activist in Montgomery, Alabama, who in 1955 refused a bus driver's order to give up her seat to a white passenger. Her act of civil disobedience became legendary in the nation's fight for integration. The trick is to look at potential leaders not solely based on their credentials, but in the discipline, values, and vision they have within.

Banking on the Future

In today's competitive marketplace, successful companies must recognize the importance of nurturing tomorrow's leaders, as they will determine the success of companies in the future. A CEO's most important responsibility is to implement a process that identifies and grooms future leaders for the organization, and to teach and mentor future leaders who exist within the company. A strong leadership pipeline perpetuates a successful company generation after generation.

Following are a few questions to think about. They're not designed to test your knowledge, and there are no right or wrong answers. Instead, it's hoped that weighing the answers will help you as an aspiring leader to understand the role and benefits of nurturing future leaders:

- Does your organization have formal leadership training for existing employees?

- What more could be done to further mentor future leaders?

- Does your company rely on bringing in outside talent to fill leadership openings? If so, can you determine why that is the case? Is there anything you can do to improve the process?

- Does an organization have to recruit "superstars" to maintain a highly successful portfolio, or can it achieve sustained top performance by maximizing the skills of its existing employees?

- What are some of the ways in which an organization can improve the performance level of its line employees?

- Think about your performance at work. Are you working to your full potential? If not, why not, and what would it take from your company or its leadership to maximize your performance level?

You Can Do It, Too

Real leadership is learned. Among the qualities that real and aspiring leaders must nurture and develop are:

- Humility.
- Quiet self-confidence (rather than boastfulness).
- Preparedness for most any situation that comes up.

- Physical, mental, and moral toughness.

- Commitment to the team as opposed to personal gain.

- Belief in the greater good and causes above self, along with a willingness to sacrifice personal gains for a greater cause.

Takeaway

- The best position for a real leader—the role that has the greatest chance of success—is as the facilitator—a trainer, teacher, and supporter who guides others and then moves aside.

- Adversity is a great motivator and teacher. Some of the greatest business leaders are people who faced adversity, failed, and then emerged stronger, wiser, and with more passion and determination to succeed.

- Leadership learning should happen at all levels of a corporation, because companies and their executives must develop an organizational culture that builds future leaders from the ground up.

- Real leaders develop a deep and wide pool of future leaders in their organization.

- Business should take a lesson from the U.S. Marines in how to build a leadership training program. The Marines teach junior officers to be strategic thinkers, to develop and execute complex plans, to supervise and motivate enlisted personnel, to be accountable for expensive equipment, and to be calm under intense pressure. Learning by doing also is a critical aspect of training, as are regular counseling, critiquing, challenging, and correcting of junior officers' performance by senior leaders.

- ◆ Employers and employees can benefit from outside and community leadership programs. Not only do the programs create a leadership pipeline, but program graduates become more effective mentors to coworkers, too.

Chapter 7

Real Leaders Know the Difference Between Character and Integrity

Integrity has no need of rules.

—Albert Camus

Real leadership is a 24/7 job that encompasses all a leader stands for and all that he or she does privately as well as publicly. Not only must a leader embody the Eight Essentials of Effective Leadership, but he or she also must be a stalwart of integrity and character. Being a real leader is a complex and challenging proposition that only the very committed can achieve successfully.

How the Mighty Have Fallen

In today's competitive marketplace, any indiscretion of character or slip-up in integrity—real or perceived by others—can seriously jeopardize the success of a company or individual. A single incident can overshadow an otherwise-stellar career and seriously damage the reputation of an organization or person, destroying years of image-building and shattering

the brand as a result. Think about how Tiger Woods dam-
aged his personal reputation and business brand because of
the highly publicized infidelities to his wife. Remember how
Toyota's stellar reputation was seemingly tarnished because
of massive, seemingly endless vehicle recalls? How does the
public view the integrity of our government after seeing one
U.S. Congressperson after another embroiled in various ethics
scandals? Remember how much heat British Petroleum took in
the wake of the Deepwater Horizon explosion and subsequent
catastrophic oil spill in the Gulf of Mexico? The reputation of
each has been severely tarnished, possibly beyond repair in
some cases.

Distant and recent history are full of missteps and hard lessons learned by individuals, companies, and corporations that
somewhere along the way failed to live up to the challenge of
maintaining strong character and sterling integrity. Some people and companies recover; some do not. For those who do recover, the process can be a long and arduous road that often
sees them falling short of past glories. That is why it is so important for businesses—large and small, and from the top leaders down—to protect their brand by preserving and fostering
the character and integrity not only of their leaders, but also of
all their employees.

Even momentary slip-ups often can derail top leaders. Paul
Levy of Harvard's medical center was a highly sought-after real
leader with impeccable character, high integrity, and across-
the-board strengths. But he momentarily lost sight of the importance of living the leadership tenets and reportedly had a
relationship with an employee that was deemed by others as inappropriate. Whatever the relationship involved, and whether
it was inappropriate or not, does not matter. Levy's troops lost
trust in him as a leader, and he eventually stepped down from
his post.

All it takes is one indiscretion to destroy—or at the very least raise problems with—the trust people have in you. As a real leader, you must never lose sight of or touch with integrity, honesty, and impeccable character. If you have any doubts about an action, don't do it, because chances are if you have doubts, so will others. And, most of all, never place yourself above and beyond those around you. You and your actions are accountable, period. Benjamin Franklin said the same thing more than 200 years ago: "It takes many good deeds to build a good reputation and only one bad one to lose it."

The Character Link

Character is the bedrock of leadership development. Those in leadership roles must have high moral standing and irreproachable ethics. After all, these leaders are charged with teaching, influencing, and molding those who work with them, for them, and around them. No one wants to lose such a position of trust because of tainted ethics and morals.

As a society, we currently place a high value on well-known personalities and celebrities. These are today's "heroes," if you will, though they often do not adhere to any moral or ethical standards of behavior. We do not require them to. But if our heroes—whose behavior we often model—fall short, we very well may fall short, too. Fortunately for all of us, true heroes still exist, though frequently lesser known, who do model admirable ethics and morals, as well as integrity, strength, and humility. It is important—for companies and individuals—not to lose sight of these lesser-known, but nonetheless true heroes and their accomplishments.

"The top three requirements of a great leader are character, character, character," says Michael Bradbury. "I know there are those who will point to former President Bill Clinton and say that he accomplished great things as president despite having affairs in the White House, so character is not important. Despite this anomaly, the public puts a high premium on integrity for its leaders...."[1]

The University of Michigan's David Brandon, whose insights you read in Chapter 5, says people are defined by the character they show during times of adversity and challenge. "It's easy to show high character when everything is going well and according to plan."[2] Whether in business, sports, or when dealing with more personal issues, a person's character is put to the test when things go wrong and the pressure mounts. The leaders I respect most are the ones who remained calm, focused, and selfless during times of duress, and made the right decisions rather than the easy or popular decisions. David Brandon once told me, "J.C. Watts had it right when he said, 'Character is doing the right thing when nobody's looking. There are too many people who think that the only thing that's right is to get by, and the only thing that's wrong is to get caught.'"[3]

The Integrity Model

Integrity is not the same as character. Every organization has its own character and culture, just as every individual has character. Character defines each of us, our values, where our moral compass lands, and how we respond when challenged by ethical conflicts. It dictates whether or not we do the right thing when no one is watching, and what principles and beliefs we endow to future generations. In short, it is who we are, and who we have the potential to be as real leaders.

Integrity is doing what you say you will do, but if you can't follow through, then admitting it to yourself and to others. "Integrity is the end result of someone who shows great character," says David Brandon. "Show me someone who is of high character, is totally honest, plays by the rules (even if he or she disagrees with them), and refuses to put their own interests ahead of others...and, I will show you someone who conducts themselves with great integrity."[4]

The Foible Factor

Real leaders, like everyone else, make mistakes. The difference between real leaders and bosses is that, although real leaders work hard to avoid mistakes, they're quick to admit when they've slipped up, and then they move on. Bosses either deny mistakes entirely or point the finger at someone else. And woe to the employee who makes a mistake; a boss isn't likely to let him or her forget it—ever.

Arnold Schwarzenegger, former governor of California, was a change maker, considered the penultimate businessman and real leader while in office. Shortly after his run as governor ended, though, he admitted to an extramarital affair and that he had fathered a child 10 years earlier during that affair. Time will tell whether his admission can repair his reputation.

During the summer of 2010, then–Detroit Tigers pitcher Armando Galarraga displayed a rare form of class, dignity, and forgiveness when he lost his bid for a perfect game against the Cleveland Indians with two outs in the top of the ninth inning. Galarraga completed the play that would have clinched his perfect game, but the umpire mistakenly called the hitter safe at first base. Rather than protesting the call or, worse, casting dispersions on the umpire, Galarraga accepted the umpire's apology. He realized that the umpire knew he had made the wrong call, which cost Galarraga his perfect game and early entry into the baseball Hall of Fame. As Galarraga later commented, "Everyone makes mistakes."

When the Truth Will Not Do

Even though truth is the guidepost and the goal, there are instances when a real leader cannot and should not always tell the whole truth. For example, if a company is getting ready to launch a new product or has a new branding strategy, exposing the launch date or the details of the strategy and its implementation could compromise or jeopardize the venture's success. If a leader is a good communicator, his or her staff will recognize the delicacy in the situation and the importance of maintaining "classified" information. However, to further ensure confidentiality, it's best to be ambiguous in reference to launch dates and other related proprietary information. Ambiguity also has a place when, for example, a CEO is interviewed on a topic that—if he or she were fully candid—could give the competition an edge. In a case like that, honesty is important, but full disclosure would be a breach of integrity.

Ventura County attorney Michael Bradbury agrees that honesty is important, above all else. "It has been my experience that being forthright with the reporter regarding the reason why you cannot fully discuss the matter is a sound approach," he says. "The experienced reporters can spot an effort to sidestep or obfuscate pretty quickly and if they believe a person is lying or being disingenuous, they typically find a way to imply in the story that the interviewee was less than cooperative/truthful.... Bottom line, being honest and up front about not being able to discuss the matter may not win you any immediate points with the reporter but he/she will continue to respect and trust you, which will pay dividends in the long run," adds Bradbury.[5]

The Less-Traveled Road

Integrity does not always mandate that a leader takes the popular approach. In fact, integrity often means just the opposite. Admiral Zumwalt personified integrity when he chose to go against convention—despite the protestation of many others in his ranks—to modernize the U.S. Navy's approach to its personnel. Harold Edwards of Limoneira chose a path unpopular with his peers when he took the helm of a company that was trying to live on past glories and opted to lead it into the 21st century by returning it to its roots of sustainability and stewardship.

As a real leader, you must be willing to assume the role of trailblazer and change agent. That means stepping out of your comfort zone and facilitating your organization's success. After carefully weighing pros and cons, real leaders will pursue a course of action because they truly believe in it—even if it's at odds with conventional wisdom. They'll also work to remove roadblocks to their team's success.

Carol Tomlinson-Keasey, founding chancellor of the University of California–Merced, was a dynamic change agent willing to tackle challenges no matter the obstacles or road-blocks in her path, and there were many formidable ones (including a battle with cancer, which she eventually lost). Her school, the 10th campus in the UC system, and the first new U.S. research university in the 21st century, is located in the San Joaquin Valley near Yosemite National Park. The fact that the campus was built is a testament to the real leadership of Tomlinson-Keasey, who needed every bit of her indefatigable spirit, positive energy, and "can-do" approach to work with three different California gubernatorial administrations and deal with controversy over the location of the campus. Many prominent Californians wanted the school in Fresno or elsewhere in the state. Construction, too, was hampered by environmental issues and limited state funding. But Tomlinson-Keasey was a real trailblazer, and the students who took her promise of higher education to heart were true pioneers. I was privileged to serve on the founding board of trustees of the University of California–Merced Foundation, and when the campus opened in 2005, it had received more endowed professorships and other large donations than many colleges that had been in existence for more than 100 years.

Take on the Tough Issues

Unlike Tomlinson-Keasey, many of today's CEOs, campus presidents, and corporate leaders shy away from the big issues and challenges. They fail to take on the controversial topics or take a stand on issues outside their organization or business. They fall short on their convictions and, in the process, they fall short as leaders. In many cases, fear of reprisal—either from the boardroom, peers, or their communities—prevents people in authority from acting boldly as real leaders. In other cases, a lack of courage undermines the will of a would-be leader.

Jackie Robinson, my first hero, did not suffer from a lack of courage and conviction. The first African-American to play Major League Baseball in the 20th century, Robinson knew no bounds when it came to leadership. He was one who led by his feats, not his mouth. He did not merely carry the torch against discrimination—he lit it.

Robinson stood tall with poise, courage, and determination while breaking the color barrier in Major League Baseball. He was constantly confronted with death threats. Opposing teams also threatened to strike because they did not want to play against his team, the Brooklyn Dodgers, who broke convention by allowing in a member who was African American. Robinson was spit on by players, and endured racial epithets from fans and players alike. His conviction—that of a real leader—was truly remarkable. It didn't take long for him to win the league over: that same year, Robinson was awarded Rookie of the Year, and just two years later he was voted baseball's Most Valuable Player. As Roger Kahn wrote in *The Boys of Summer*, Jackie Robinson "bore the burden of a pioneer and the weight made him stronger."[6]

But even Robinson did not do it alone. Harold "Pee Wee" Reese, the Dodgers' shortstop, team captain, and another of my early heroes, stood shoulder to shoulder with Robinson when the going got tough. Together he and Robinson were a project team with plenty of pennant success to their credit. During one especially raucous game in 1947, Reese (whose southern roots were in Louisville, Kentucky) put his arm around Robinson in front of the crowd to show the world his acceptance and support for his rookie teammate.

Robinson's character was of such impressive quality that he was posthumously awarded both the Presidential Medal of Freedom and the Congressional Gold Medal—not too shabby for a guy who played baseball for a living!

Real leaders like Jackie Robinson have a lasting impact inside their organizations and often on the public stage outside their institutions. That is a measure of their success. Those impacts come from the creation of an ongoing culture of real leaders, as a result of their actions, and in changes—large or small—that live well past their tenure with an organization.

Beyond Minor Slip-Ups

Trust is what makes a team work. A combination of integrity and character, trust is essential to organizational success. Without the forward momentum that comes with trust, progress grinds quickly to a halt.

History may judge 2008 and 2009 (2010 and 2011 may qualify, too) as "The Scandal Years"—the period of time that shattered the capitalistic bubble, and left the rest of the leadership world with the daunting challenge of how to rebuild trust in capitalism and business. What could have so thoroughly influenced the American corporation's fall from grace? A series of boss-like actions committed by leaders are in large part to blame. They include:

- ◆ John Thain, former CEO of Merrill Lynch who resigned in 2009, spent more than $1 million renovating his personal office while the company hemorrhaged.

- New York Gov. Eliot Spitzer resigned under threat of impeachment in 2008 after first denying, and then admitting, that he patronized a high-priced prostitution ring.

- American International Group (AIG), after receiving an $85 billion bailout from the U.S. government in 2008—only the first installment of a cash infusion of more than $180 billion—sent its top sales performers to a lavish resort weekend. Days later, it came out that the Federal Reserve provided this company with an additional $37 billion. As of the end of May 2011, the company was still struggling.

- Presidential hopeful and former U.S. Sen. John Edwards denied, then later admitted to, an extramarital affair while his wife was battling breast cancer. He later blamed his hubris for his indiscretion and described his attitude as a "self-focus, an egotism, a narcissism that leads you to believe that you can do whatever you want...and there will be no consequences."[7] His wife legally separated from him in 2008, and two years later died of cancer.

- In 2009, Bernard Madoff, a once-prominent broker, pleaded guilty to masterminding a more-than-$60-billion Ponzi scheme—the largest in history—that defrauded thousands of investors. He is now serving out his 150-year prison sentence.

And, unfortunately, the list goes on and on.

The biggest losers in the wake of all these scandals are the workers and participants, whose trust in the leadership of America has been shattered. The current recession, along with its accompanying massive unemployment, has exacerbated this loss of trust. In order for an economic recovery to truly take hold, real leaders must restore trust, or at least a portion of it.

When trust pervades a workplace, it fosters higher performance, reduces operational costs, eliminates needless litigation, and retains the most productive workers. A workplace filled with trust also perpetuates the most desirable aspects of a company's culture, nurtures an *esprit de corps,* and sustains financial success, especially in times of unprecedented, complex change. All of these building blocks for a successful organization are sorely lacking in much of today's workforce.

Rx for Rebuilding

Real leaders must face up to this lack of trust, and make a commitment to rebuilding and reconstruction. A commitment to perhaps try one thing new each week, or even daily, can go a long way toward making a difference. The real leaders' prescription to restore employee trust includes:

- ✦ Hiring CEOs on the basis of their moral fiber in addition to the regular prerequisites that executive search firms and boards of directors jointly identify. Companies must scrutinize potential candidates with the same conviction and high standards as is required for White House Cabinet officers and justices of the Supreme Court, and ensure that the organization's board of directors more closely monitors and objectively evaluates the CEO's behavior, as well as his or her performance on the job and off.

- ✦ Practicing President Ronald Reagan's signature phrase from the Russian proverb "trust, but verify." We have all seen too many examples where boards abdicated their governance roles and, as such, their roles as corporate "watchdogs." The board practice of basing CEO compensation on "benchmarking" other CEOs' salaries and benefits rather than on their company's performance is also much too prevalent today.

- ◆ Realigning compensation programs so that the wide gulf that now exists between executives and rank-and-file workers is narrowed. Companies must insist that CEOs demonstrate transparency and function as authentic leaders who genuinely value their employees as partners. CEOs can accomplish this goal by consistent actions that through time demonstrate their commitment to their employees.

- ◆ Harboring no hidden agendas, sharing information as fully and as broadly as possible, and remembering that there is no such thing as a private conversation. In other words, companies must give the same information to each of their constituencies, and never say anything that they would not want repeated.

- ◆ Owning up to their mistakes and informing others of them up front.

The Truth About Credibility

Core values such as honor, service, and teamwork are too often absent in today's work setting. If the words sound familiar, that is because they are leadership qualities taught by the U.S. Marines—that top-notch training I talked about previously. Add to those values the core tenet of honesty. Together they lend credibility to real leaders. Honesty goes well beyond the spoken word. Often the nonverbal cues from individuals and bosses or leaders are as important as the verbal ones. Real leaders are humble and compassionate in their actions, yet steadfast in their words. Real leaders will look you directly in the eyes when talking to you; they are just as unwavering in their pursuit of their ideals and beliefs.

♦

Take the truth or consequences test: Next time someone talks to you—especially if he or she is giving out directions—notice if he or she looks you directly in the eyes. If not, one has to wonder if he or she is telling the truth. Real leaders are frank and unwavering.

♦

Cues and Values

Be sure whatever nonverbal cues you're sending or receiving are in line with your core values and the tenets of real leadership. If they're not, figure out why not, and work hard to align both. You'll be more consistent in what you say and do, and those who interact with you will appreciate your steadfast consistency—whether they realize it or not.

Too many people write performance reviews that aren't helpful because they aren't fully truthful. Whenever a performance review is perfunctory, vindictive, or somewhere in between, chances are it was written by someone who thinks as a boss, not a leader. A real leader will take the time for honest and open communication, will get to know his or her employees, and will not compromise his or her character or integrity by fabricating or "fudging" something as important as a performance review. After all, if a leader is doing his or her job of teaching and mentoring tomorrow's leaders, a performance review will be honest and constructive, and will offer real direction for the employee.

Too many grades are awarded to students who have not earned their marks. Too many testimonials are written by people who should have declined being used as a reference. Once again, it is the honest and open communication of real leaders that offers the valuable lessons that help others succeed.

Politics and Principles

One of the U.S. Senate's most principled solons is Sen. Carl Levin. I helped campaign for him, contributed to his reelections, and served on his Military Academies Selection Committee. Like his esteemed brother, Rep. Sander (Sandy) Levin, who serves in a leadership role in the House of Representatives, Sen. Levin has steadfastly stuck to his principles. Among his many accomplishments, several characteristics serve as examples of his rare blend of leadership:

- A fighter for heightened ethics in government.
- A staunch trailblazer for removing waste in government spending.
- An advocate for manufacturing to enable our country to compete more effectively on the world stage.
- A defender of a vigilant and strong national security apparatus.

In everything he undertakes, Sen. Levin does his homework, pays great attention to detail, and always displays a keen understanding of the subjects being discussed in the halls of Congress.

You Gotta Believe!

The heart of leadership is believing in yourself and your vision, and in turn motivating others to follow you. Real and effective leaders also live and practice the following:

- **Humanity, love of people, honesty, and hard work.** Consider leaders like Fred Meijer, the CEO of

Michigan-based Meijer superstores, who always would arrive at work early and end his day well after dark. In between he always took time for whatever was required of him—and what was not, including greeting his customers and employees.

- ◆ **Perseverance and never giving up.** The Baltimore Colts Marching Band is a great example of unrelenting purpose and resolve. In 1984, when the Colts franchise was sold to Indianapolis, the band would not go. Instead, its members—loyal to the city and each other—had other ideas. In the wee hours of the morning when the Colts began their infamous move to Indianapolis, the band members managed to remove their equipment before the moving vans arrived, and they were able to get their uniforms from the dry cleaner and hide them in a member's cemetery vault until the franchise gave them permission to keep them. The band's incredible dedication and moxie during the next 12 years helped persuade the Maryland legislature to fund a new football stadium, and that finally brought the Ravens franchise to Baltimore in 1996.

- ◆ **Vision, a highly developed strategic orientation, the courage of conviction, and a devotion to country and public service.** Retired four-star Gen. Anthony C. "Tony" Zinni is a true visionary who never stops serving others. The former Marine now is chairman of the board of directors of BAE Systems, Inc., an international multi-billion-dollar conglomerate, as well as an in-demand motivational and leadership speaker. His nearly 40-year, highly decorated military career included a tour as commander in chief of the U.S. Central Command at the Pentagon. Since retiring, his endeavors have included serving as U.S. Peace Envoy to the Middle East and Special Envoy to the Henri Dunant Centre for Humanitarian Dialogue (Indonesia, Philippines, and Sudan peace effort).

All of us, leaders included, learn from experiences, trial and error, leadership simulations, field testing, "live fire," and mentorship. It all begins with a positive attitude—yours as well as that of your leaders and mentors.

David Brandon shares this lasting advice that served him well throughout his illustrious career:

> The best lesson in character and integrity was taught to me by my father when I received my first promotion early in my career. I was taking over a unit that had several people who were going to be working for me that were old enough to be my father and much more experienced in the business than I was at the time. I asked him (my father) for his advice, and he replied, "Well Dave, I have never been in the situation you now find yourself, but if I were you, I would find out how people want to be treated, and treat them that way." Very good advice from a very wise man.[8]

Can You Cut It?

The success of any team or enterprise depends, in part, on the leader's ability to earn the trust of his or her employees. Yet study after study reports declining loyalty all around us. The trust must be rebuilt to ensure solid economic regrowth. Real leaders recognize the need to restore trust, and they invest in the time and effort needed to do so. Is trust missing in the workplace at your company? If so, why? What can be done to foster trust in your workplace?

To rebuild trust demands the initiatives of real leadership. Concrete steps that those in positions of leadership can take to help foster trust include:

- Recognizing the accomplishments and successes of others.

- Hiring management and leaders based on abilities, ethics, and morals.

- Investing in fail-safes to make sure management actually lives up to expectations.

- Instituting performance-based compensation.

- Being open, honest, and up-front with employees.

- Admitting your mistakes rather than passing the buck.

Many successful leaders can achieve even greater results if they become stronger change agents—if they learn how to develop stronger alliances, coalitions, partnerships, and connections with others. How would you rate your own ability to mobilize widespread support for the initiatives that are important to you? How can you improve on that ability? Are you passionate enough about those initiatives? What else can you do to strengthen strategic alliances and gain widespread support?

The next time you are in a position to rally the troops, think about how important it is to believe in what you're doing and how you're doing it. If you do not believe in yourself and your mission, how can you expect others to believe in you?

When you fail in something or don't live up to expectations—yours or someone else's—what do you do? Do you quickly move on, or do you stop, assess what happened, determine the mistakes that were made by you or someone else, figure out what could have been done differently to improve the outcome, and then move on? Real leader or not, we're all supposed to learn from our mistakes in whatever we do. In fact, even with positive outcomes, it is important to review the steps and actions that led to that success and analyze what could have been done differently to further improve on the outcome.

How can overcoming adversity or rebounding from it help shape an emerging leader's skill set? What can you learn from your mistakes and your successes? In the context of leadership, what are some of the mistakes you have made in the past? Write them down, then think about how you might have handled the situation differently to prevent or avoid the mistake, or at least lessen its negative impact.

You Can Do It, Too

To further entrench your own real leadership, believe in yourself and what you can accomplish, then passionately follow the credo of service above self, empowerment and not control, and serving rather than being served. Forget garnering the "atta boys" for yourself; pursue them for your team members and their projects instead.

Listen to the views, perspectives, and opinions of those around you, too. They are invaluable in forming your own perspective. In that vein, surround yourself with people who excel in areas you do not, and don't hire "yes" men or "yes" women, but be confident and trust in your own judgment—your gut feelings. Utilizing actionable data before making decisions is great, but also appreciate that too much data may lessen the need for your good judgment.

Be diligent in hiring new staff, too. Avoid people who are always negative, are circumventers, or may try to undermine team efforts. If despite your best efforts, you find yourself working with someone like this, have the guts—the real leadership—to admit your mistake and correct it.

Takeaway

- Character is the bedrock of leadership development.

- Real leaders take on the tough issues and challenges, and are not afraid to stand up for their values and beliefs, no matter how unpopular. Be leery of the executive who is conflict averse. Conflict, when channeled effectively, is often a positive change-maker.

- Real leaders practice core values like honesty and integrity.

- When leaders believe in themselves and their visions, others are motivated to follow.

- Real leaders must work to rebuild employee trust. To do that requires a commitment to hiring based on skill levels; compensation that's fair and equitable for everyone; an honest and straightforward approach; and in case of mistakes, owning up and moving on. (For excellent articles on the subject of trust, its restoration, and the importance in organizational life today, see articles written by Ross Goldberg, president, Kevin/Ross Public Relations.)[9]

Chapter 8

Get Ready to Lead

An army of a thousand is easy to find, but, ah,
how difficult to find a general.
—Chinese Proverb

In these pages you have read about some of the admirable leaders of yesterday and today, and the traits that make them great. Whether leaders of countries, mega-corporations, the military, or small businesses, each individual in his or her own way makes a difference and inspires those around him or her to achieve greatness.

The choice is now yours. Are you ready to step out from the shadows and step up to the challenge to inspire others, to promote your passions, to recommit to your ideals, and to become one of tomorrow's real leaders? The choice is not easy. Not everyone is comfortable in a leadership role or cut out to be a real leader in the workplace. Almost all of us, however, can become better people in our work and personal lives by adopting some or all of the qualities that characterize real leaders.

Don't be discouraged if you feel as if your path to leadership is stymied by too many roadblocks, potholes, and distractions. If you commit to becoming a better person, a better leader, you have a better chance to succeed. As I mentioned previously, many of the great leaders of yesterday and today faced big obstacles to their leadership, yet they persevered in their convictions, and went on to become great. You can do it, too.

Great Political Leaders and Teachers

Aspiring leaders today would do well to follow the examples of former U.S. President Ronald Reagan and Sen. Edward M. Kennedy. Both were great men who were friends despite their very different political beliefs and, as real leaders, did not allow their egos to get in the way of their work. Reagan and Kennedy were not afraid to hire staffs that were brighter or more capable than they were in some capacities, and the staffers were incredibly loyal. And, this is certainly true in my case as well, as each one of my team members was more talented than me. Few would dispute that Sen. Kennedy had one of the most talented congressional staffs in recent history.

Veterans of Kennedy's Senate staff and Reagan's White House often went on to become illustrious alumni. A few of those proud former staffers include Melody Barnes, former chief counsel to Sen. Kennedy, and now President Obama's top domestic advisor; Kenneth R. Feinberg, Kennedy's former chief of staff who served in the Obama administration as the "pay czar" or Special Master for TARP Executive Compensation; Supreme Court Chief Justice John Roberts, a former associate counsel to Reagan; and Peggy Noonan, Reagan's speechwriter and special assistant, now a *New York Times* best-selling author and conservative columnist.

◆

"Surround yourself with the best people you can find, delegate authority, and don't interfere as long as the policy you've decided upon is being carried out."[1]

—President Ronald Reagan

◆

U.S. Sen. Richard Lugar is another who is a highly talented, true servant leader, one who develops others, and someone for whom I've also campaigned several times. A former Rhodes Scholar, former mayor of Indianapolis, and former chairman of the Senate Foreign Relations Committee, he wields considerable influence in Indiana, Washington, D.C., and the nation. But as I said earlier, he's humble, approachable, and a dedicated teacher. Lugar makes a strong commitment to build leaders from the ground up, to build consensus, and to remain committed to his beliefs. His work will live on long after he leaves Congress. It certainly did in Indianapolis, where as mayor he transformed city government through creation of "Unigov," at the time a controversial move to combine the city and county into one governmental entity. Despite opposition, Lugar was steadfast in his belief that Indianapolis and the surrounding area needed to broaden its population and tax base in order to attract new business and develop into a world-class city.

Lugar's myriad accomplishments are testaments to his consistent drive to build consensus. He's a leader who believes in reason and sharing information. Even in the heat of a tough political campaign, Sen. Lugar has the ability to take a negative question and turn it into an opportunity to bring people to his point of view. He allows for a critic's doubt, calmly explains why the criticism is not accurate, and then enlightens the audience with more information, often letting them inside the complex process of making an important decision.

Seeking his seventh consecutive term, the Hoosier icon is one of the Senate's brightest, most savvy, conscientious, trustworthy, pragmatic, and farsighted public servants. When I heard recently that some have criticized him for having "crossed the aisle" to work with Democrats to pass critically important legislation, I was reminded of great Americans like Sam Rayburn of Texas, Mike Mansfield of Montana, Howard Baker of Tennessee, and Philip Hart of Michigan—who also put country above party and self. I have often asked myself what experiences were pivotal in Lugar's development as a real leader. Was it being a farmer, business owner, naval officer, or mayor of a major city? Perhaps it is the combination of these and other experiences, his family, and more that led *Time* magazine to name Lugar as one of America's 10 best Senators. Lugar's courage and willingness to risk his own political future for the sake of the country make him my pick for a real leader.

Beyond Politics

If more CEOs, college presidents, hospital administrators, and elected officials followed these examples of placing a premium on finding and nurturing top talent—their individual performance and that of their organizations would improve immeasurably. What these real leaders recognized is that if you deliberately hire the best talent, mentor them, and reward them, then others among the best and the brightest talent also will want to work for you.

Leland Doan, Dow Chemical CEO, used his unique brand of quiet diplomacy as a bridge between the old and emerging leaders of the company, and thus positioned Dow for greatness going forward. As author Don Whitehead writes in *The Dow Story: The History of Dow Chemical Company* (McGraw-Hill, 1983), Doan led "the company over the postwar shoals into its greatest period of growth in its history." Do you really believe that one of a real leader's most important roles is not to develop a leadership pipeline within the organization? At one time, Dow boasted of having more individuals with doctoral degrees on its payroll than any company or university in the country.

In sports, John Wooden, Mike Krzyzewski, Nick Saban, and Bo Schembechler are excellent examples of real leaders who could and did draw from a ready supply of athletes clamoring to be part of the team. None of these outstanding leaders ever bossed, but they were definitely disciplined; indeed, they are examples for trying to teach athletes much more than the X's and O's of basketball and football, and many of the young men they mentored are champions in all aspects of life.

Tough Leaders for Tough Times

Recently, I had the privilege of meeting Gen. Tony Zinni, highly decorated retired U.S. Marine, former CENTCOM commander in chief, diplomat, presidential advisor, and confidant to several corporate CEOs. Zinni, along with Tony Koltz, recently authored *Leading the Charge: Leadership Lessons from the Battlefield to the Boardroom* (Palgrave McMillan, 2009).

Zinni says that there is a "deep desire among Americans for true leadership in troubled and confusing times." He states that "the new leader must be able to operate at a blisteringly fast pace and be quick to harness ever-evolving technologies."[2] If Zinni and others are correct in these assessments, that a major reordering of the world is occurring and that we are experiencing a "shake-up" like no other, it is clear that we need leaders who have the ability and toughness to place things in proper perspective and the perseverance to get up after being knocked down, be stronger than before, and succeed.

Leaders Anywhere, Anytime

Real leaders aren't found only in the military, Congress, or the C-suite. Each of us can be the captain of our own veritable ship and an inspiration to those around us anywhere, anytime, and in any situation.

Consider the case of two volunteers. Mike Andres of Simi Valley, California, is an individual who, as a volunteer, is a real leader to those around him. He's not CEO of The Biggest Company in the World. Until recently, he served as a volunteer hole captain of the Northern Trust–sponsored Los Angeles Open golf tournament's special marshals. His role was to ensure that decorum wass maintained at all times during the tournament on the links at the Riviera Country Club.

Andres always took his job as a volunteer very seriously. He kept his team of volunteers informed via phone calls prior to the local tournament, with e-mail updates about participating golfers—stars and otherwise—and through other forms of communication. Beyond the basics, Andres made sure participants understood the mission of the tournament, were acquainted with the charities that benefit from tournament proceeds, and knew what was expected of them as marshals. He also carefully outlined possible expectations in terms of various participating golfers' preferences, issues, and idiosyncrasies. His goal, like that of the CEO of a major company, was to make sure his team knew the players, what to expect, and how to react to whatever situation might arise.

Ed Pagliasotti, a retired Air Force colonel, is another volunteer and real leader to others. He is the volunteer head of the Retired Activities Office at Naval Base Ventura County. His job is, in part, to develop other volunteers who can then ably assist former military personnel and their family members to navigate the military bureaucracy and receive the services they have earned.

He, too, takes his unpaid job very seriously and works diligently to maintain high standards amid what can be overwhelming layers of government bureaucracy. Despite the many challenges, Pagliasotti maintains his sense of humor and steadfast determination and direction. His commitment to personal quality and service is unforgettable.

In the workplace, commitment makes a difference, too. Years ago when I took over as chief of public relations at Blue Shield of California, the company and the healthcare industry were in turmoil. The San Francisco–based healthcare company had been around for nearly 75 years, but over the years its brand had lost some of its luster.

My goal was to enhance the integrity and brand of the company by boosting its visibility. We wanted Blue Shield to be instantly recognizable as delivering superior value and service to its customers. The solution, my team determined, was to partner with a highly visible, highly respected community leader—in this case, the San Francisco Giants baseball club. The partnership would include advertising at Pacific Bell Park (now AT&T Park) and promoting the Giants' and Blue Shield's anti-domestic violence campaign. It was a new and different approach for the health insurer, and initially the top leaders were opposed to the initiative. But I was convinced it was a good fit and a necessary alliance that would re-invigorate the brand by enhancing the organization's image in the city and across the state. It also would create a positive partnership with a very popular organization, the San Francisco Giants, one built around the prevention of domestic violence. Senior management at Blue Shield eventually agreed to the alliance, and 10 years later, the program is still going strong and so is Blue Shield. Mario Alioto, the Giants' superb corporate marketing vice president with whom I worked directly for many consecutive weeks to develop a mutually acceptable proposal, became a close friend in this process of "shuttle diplomacy" between our companies. He, too, is a real leader.

Relationship Wisdom

As former U.S. Defense Secretary Robert Gates so aptly demonstrated in his tenure under both the Bush and Obama administrations, leadership is so much about relationships. To accomplish goals, to get things done in the government, in the workplace, and in your life, requires alliances with others. Without them, success—if achieved at all—will be short-lived. In other words, leaders can't go it alone. It takes troops who understand your vision to help achieve your goals. It's interesting to note that many leading business schools have only recently begun to realize the importance of experiential learning, critical skill development, and "people skills." Learning how to effectively work with others has never been more important.

As a real leader you must have a keen desire to listen to all the stakeholders, starting with employees. CEOs must recognize that they can learn from interactions with employees and other key shareholders. The interaction, especially if frequent enough, instills two-way trust and the leader's vision is made real to all.

The Family Model

Many lessons from the workplace are interchangeable with the experiences in raising a family. As Amway co-founder and NBA Orlando Magic owner Rich DeVos said, "Leadership *is* what you do at home." DeVos is a gifted leader who is certainly no stranger to adversity, having overcome many challenges on his way to the top of the business world. He's a man of great faith, an indefatigable cheerleader, and an articulate and staunch champion of the free enterprise system.

My wife, Joan, and I received similar good advice from our minister, who performed our wedding ceremony many years ago. He advised us to model leadership in our lives, to read books on marriage and then discuss them, never to go to bed angry with your spouse (both of us having had our share of yawningly long hours at work the next day because of it), and to reach agreement on our respective life goals before our wedding. He was a firm believer that each one of us needed to make a 150-percent effort in order for our union to survive and blossom.

Neither of us really used the terms *leadership* or *public service* to shape our discussion of the fundamentals of the kind of home we hoped to establish, nor was the term used in either of our parents' homes. But leadership and public service were more than abundant in Joan's home and in mine; they just weren't labeled as such.

We established several ground rules that we would strive to live by. They included:

◆ **Having a game plan** (what many organizations typically refer to as their "vision" and "strategy"). It consisted of a few foundations: to agree on the part of the country we wanted to live in where there was heterogeneity, diversity, and a good college because lifelong learning was an integral part of our ethos; to select a community where we could afford to live and participate actively; to get to know one another better before we started a family (which we would do four years later); and to share our experiences and our love with each other at the end of our respective workdays.

◆ **Setting a high moral standard** (businesses often call this their integrity or ethical principles). We strived to set a high standard of regularly practicing our faith, remaining active in a denomination of our choosing when we began a family, and raising our children in the church because we believed it provided a key part of the foundation for a strong, healthy family.

♦ **Creating family traditions** (organizations sometimes call this corporate culture). We wanted to instill in our children an appreciation of people different from them; to broaden their and our knowledge of the arts, literature, and history; and to visit much of the United States and other countries. It was important that our children learn self-discipline, respect for others, proper etiquette, and how to overcome adversity, for experiencing some failure is an effective teacher and builder of strong character and resiliency. We also believed it was vital to our sons' development that they learn to love, have fun, be positive, be thankful for what they have, and assist others less fortunate.

♦ **Developing skills for success** (some businesses call this focus, execution, and risk-taking). We believed that our children needed to learn to be independent thinkers, self-sufficient, broad-minded, and secular as well as religious. We strived to expose them to people who were intellectually curious, who were well read and whose views weren't necessarily the same as ours. We also wanted them to have heroes— people they had read about or had seen—who were inspiring, courageous, and worth looking up to. The phrase "Mom (or Dad), I'm bored" was never tolerated in our home. We used books, Boy Scouts, athletics, concerts, art galleries, lectures, travel, friendships from various faiths, and numerous family discussions to broaden their horizons and keep them occupied.

We had often talked about how best to prepare our children to enable them to hopefully reach their full potential. I'll never forget when my wife shared a quote with me from Alabama's legendary head football coach, Paul "Bear" Bryant, that in a few words captured many of the lessons we tried to teach our children: "It's not the will to win that matters—everyone has that. It's the will to prepare to win that matters."

◆

"We make a living by what we get; we make a life by what we give."[3]

—Sir Winston Churchill

◆

Leadership Wisdom

Now it is your turn to take the lead, to position yourself to become a real leader. Remember that the methods of leadership may change from place to place, and different leaders offer their own style of leadership. But one thing remains a constant: leaders must find ways to inspire their team if they, their people, and their companies are to succeed. Here are a few more leadership thoughts gleaned from years in the trenches that may help you grow your own leadership skills the right way:

- ◆ **On hiring:** Before hiring an individual, ask yourself: "Is this the kind of person I would want to be in a foxhole with?" If the answer is no, it may be best to pass on hiring the person. After all, leadership success is a team effort. Everyone on the team must be able to sacrifice, work together, and do so closely.

- ◆ **On firing:** Firing is a last resort after every other change effort has failed. Genuinely help the person find a position elsewhere where there is a better fit. For the good of other staff or the organization as a whole, terminating an employee is sometimes the only alternative.

- ◆ **On team-building:** Building the right team, and giving each team member clear roles and responsibilities that match their skills, is an essential part of the leadership role in whatever you do.

- ◆ **On change:** Real leadership implies change— change that moves the organization forward in strategic ways to achieve its overarching goals. Effective leadership forecasts that needed change will occur and that it will improve the organization's fortunes.

- ◆ **On countermoves:** Leaders must be like good quarterbacks, in that they need to see the field ahead of them, anticipate what linebackers and defensive backs are going to do, and have an audible they can call before the snap to counter their likely moves. That's one reason current and former senior enlisted personnel and officers in the military often make good leaders: they're taught the art of strategy better than most.

- ◆ **On honesty:** Michael Bradbury emphasizes the importance of honesty: "If I've learned anything, it is to be 100 percent honest and forthcoming. The public forgives a mistake but never forgets or forgives an attempt to cover up the mistake."[4]

- ◆ **On greater achievements:** Passion and pride drive teams to excellence. Committed team members who believe in their goals and their leaders' vision realize the need to get better, achieve more, and gain broader recognition and success for their organization. They also want to set an example others can emulate, follow, and adapt.

♦ **On the Golden Rule:** A real leader is always kind and considerate of others, regardless of his or her position or station.

Beyond Compensation

How will you, as a leader, inspire and motivate others? That is up to you. I've tried to provide a backbone of understanding from what four decades of studying and working with real leaders has taught me. Real leaders adhere 24/7 to all of the Eight Essentials of Effective Leadership—including honesty, integrity, vision, passion, commitment, communication, and accessibility. But to infuse others with the excitement that's required for long-term team success also demands recognition of employee successes.

Cash for performance is great, but often a leader can't offer monetary rewards for a job well done. As effective, if not more so, is a personal note of congratulations or thanks. It is that recognition for a job well done that you read about in Chapter 2 that is important to Millennials in today's workplace. It is as important to all generations of workers, too.

For many years, I've been using a 3.5 inch by 5.5 inch card with two signal flags and the words *Bravo Zulu* below the flags to commend members of my team and others in the organization who achieve something especially noteworthy. "Bravo Zulu," in Navy jargon, means "well done." On the back side of the card, I write a handwritten note. It's personal, congratulatory, unexpected, and appreciated. A word of warning, however:

Bravo Zulu

A black and white version of the Bravo Zulu "Job Well Done" cards.

don't hand out the recognitions too frequently or foolishly, or their effect will be diluted.

Bill Caudill, patriarch of the architectural firm Caudill Rowlett Scott of Houston, Texas, used his own interpretation of my Bravo Zulu card. Caudill used a pocket-sized card emblazoned with the firm's logo to deliver personal congratulations to members of the firm who had done exemplary work. He used a combination of words and cartoonish pictures to convey his message. Each card was delightfully and personally unique. As such, employees tacked them up in their workstations, almost as military personnel might display their medals.

You Can Do It, Too

Cookie-cutter leadership—like cookie-cutter leaders—doesn't work. Every real leader is unique in his or her own way—in style, in approach, in attitude. What is universal, though, is the strong commitment and intense passion that real leaders have for the job at hand, no matter how big or small it may be. One of the biggest mistakes of aspiring leaders is to think that all he or she has to do is the same thing as some other leader. Patterning your leadership style after another does not make you an effective leader. Be yourself and allow the passion for what you do to come through.

Each of us can become a real leader by observing other (good and bad) leaders, and by reading and studying what works and what does not work with the help of real-life practice and experience. Watch the workings in your own company, turn on the TV or radio, or pick up your handheld and listen to and watch the interactions of others in the news. Study political jockeying in the news. What actions, attitudes, or approaches propel someone ahead or force someone else to concede and why? It's all a valuable study in leadership or lack thereof, and you can learn from it.

Make a list and write down what you consider the most important tenets of your leadership style. Then, make a list of what you regard as others' most remarkable leadership traits. Read both lists and then think about how you do or do not live up to those aspirations. And, yes, don't forget to make a third list of those traits you don't admire but have observed in others in positions of responsibility, so you can avoid those characteristics at all costs. If you come up short in one area, ask yourself what you can do to improve. Continue to add to these lists, as they will help be your guide to developing your leadership skills as one of tomorrow's leaders. Keep in mind, too, the tenents of servant leadership we've talked about throughout this book. A servant leader doesn't think in terms of having subordinates or followers. He or she is a champion for the team and always promotes and helps them. He or she sets the most enviable example and demonstrates by his or her character what serving others really means.

Takeaway

- Don't allow obstacles to stand in the way of achievement. Real leaders learn how to overcome obstacles, to grow from the experiences, and to flourish.

- Each of us is the CEO of our own life and can achieve great things with the right attitude, approach, and outlook. Steve Jobs, the late, extraordinary, and pioneering co-founder of Apple, once said, "Your time is limited, so don't waste it living someone else life."[5]

- Leaders cannot go it alone. It takes a troop that understands your vision to help achieve your goals.

- Real leaders must inspire those around them to achieve lasting success.

- Real leaders adhere 24/7 to all of the Eight Essentials of Effective Leadership, and, to infuse others with the excitement that's required for long-term team success, they pay attention to and recognize employee successes.

- Real leaders do not allow their egos to get in the way of the task at hand.

Notes

Chapter 1

1. "I Can't Get No...Job Satisfaction, That Is," The Conference Board (January 2010), *www.conference-board.org/publications/publicationdetail.cfm?publicationid=1727* (accessed February 2, 2011).

2. "Fueling Business Growth Number One Issue for CEOs," The Conference Board (April 12, 2011), *www.conference-board.org/press/pressdetail.cfm?pressid=4167* (accessed February 2, 2011).

3. "Leaders in the Crisis: McKinsey Global Survey Results," *McKinsey Quarterly* (August 2009), *www.mckinseyquarterly.com/article_print.aspx?L2=1&L3=105&ar=2422* (Accessed February 2, 2011).

4. Barack Obama. Remarks in an address to the nation on Libya. (March 28, 2011), National Defense University, *www.whitehouse.gov/the-press-office/2011/03/28/remarks-president-address-nation-libya* (accessed April 1, 2011).

5. Cynthia Furlong Reynolds, *Jiffy: A Family Tradition* (Chelsea, Mich.: Chelsea Milling Company, 2008).

6. Scott Monty, "Ford CEO: 14 Lessons in Leadership & Marketing," The Social CMO Blog (February 13, 2010), *www.thesocialcmo.com/blog/2010/02/ford-ceo-14-lessons-in-leadership-marketing* (accessed July 27, 2011).

7. "Researchers Make Link Between Bad Bosses and Workers' Heart Disease," Stockholm University press release (January 7, 2009), *www.su.se/english/about/news-and-events/researchers-make-link-between-bad-bosses-and-workers-heart-disease-1.1044* (accessed April 7, 2011).

8. Michael Bradbury. Interview with author, May 24, 2011.

9. Pat Williams, *The Paradox of Power* (New York: First Warner Books, 2002).

10. "Old vs. New Forms of Leadership: Comparison between traditional and collaborative leadership behaviors," Wisconsin Leadership Institute Collaborative Leadership Network (July 2011), *www.leadershipskillsandvalues.com/clnontheweb-curriculum/old-vs-new-leadership* (accessed July 27, 2011).

11. Michael Bradbury. Interview with author, May 24, 2011.

12. Ron Alsop, *The Trophy Kids Grow Up* (San Francisco, Calif.: Jossey-Bass, 2008).

13. "Sixth Annual Hay Group Study Identifies Best Companies for Leadership," Hay Group press release (January 25, 2011), *www.haygroup.com/ww/press/Details.aspx?ID=28838* (accessed February 2, 2011).

14. Harold Edwards. Interview with author, May 23, 2011.

Chapter 2

1. "Sixth Annual Hay Group Study Identifies Best Companies for Leadership," Hay Group press release (January 25, 2011), *www.haygroup.com/ww/press/Details.aspx?ID=28838* (accessed February 2, 2011).

2. "About Zumwalt," Thurman Zumwalt Foundation, *http://tzfoundation.org/zumwalt.html* (accessed April 25, 2011).

3. "FAQ: Z-grams: A List of Policy Directives Issued by Admiral Zumwalt While in Office as Chief of Naval Operations, 1 July 1970 to 1 July 1974," Naval History & Heritage Command, *www.history.navy.mil/faqs/faq93-2.htm* (accessed July 27, 2011).

4. Sen. Russell Feingold. U.S. Congressional Record—Senate (January 24, 2000), *www.gpo.gov/fdsys/pkg/CRECB-2000-pt1/pdf/CRECB-2000-pt1-Pg44-3.pdf* (accessed April 25, 2011).

5. William J. Clinton. Remarks at Admiral Zumwalt Memorial Service (January 10, 2000), *http://archives.clintonpresidentialcenter.org/?u=011000-speech-by-president-at-admiral-zumwalt-memorial-service.htm* (accessed April 27, 2011).

6. Harold Edwards. Interview with author, May 23, 2011.

7. Harold Edwards. Interview with author, April 2009.

8. Michael Bradbury. Interview with author, May 24, 2011.

9. "The Millennials: A Portrait of Generation Next," Pew Research Center (updated May 26, 2011), *http://pewresearch.org/millennials*.

10. Michael Bradbury. Interview with author, May 24, 2011.

11. Mark VanderKlipp. Interview with author, July 3, 2011.

Chapter 3

1. B.L. Ochman, "Survey: Only 2% of Execs Write Their Own Blogs. That's Simply Dishonest!" What's Next Blog, *www.whatsnextblog.com/2006/01/survey_only_2_of_execs_write_t/* (accessed May 2010).

2. Dennis Sparks, "Leaning Forward, Explain, Inspire, Lead: An Interview with Noel Tichy," *National Development Council* 26:2, *www.learningforward.org/news/jsd/tichy262.cfm* (accessed July 27, 2011).

3. Colin Powell. *Stanford Report* (November 30, 2005), *http://news.stanford.edu/news/2005/november30/powell-113005.html*.

4. "The Ray Kroc Story," *www.mcdonalds.com/us/en/our_story/our_history/the_ray_kroc_story.html* (accessed April 5, 2011).

Chapter 4

1. Larry Ames. Interview with the author, May 8, 2011.

2. "History," Doug Flutie Jr. Foundation for Autism, *www.dougflutiejrfoundation.org/About-The-Foundation-History.asp* (accessed April 6, 2011).

3. Harold Edwards. Interview with author, April 2009.

4. Judith Rodin, *The University and Urban Revival: Out of the Ivory Tower and Into the Streets* (Philadelphia, Penn.: University of Pennsylvania Press, 2007), *www.upenn.edu/pennpress/book/14337.html* (accessed April 6, 2011).

5. Ibid.

6. "President Steven B. Sample to Retire in August," *USC News* (November 1, 2009), *http://uscnews.usc.edu/university/uscs_steven_sample_announces_retirement_as_president_effective_august_2_2010.html* (accessed April 7, 2011).

7. Timm Herdt, "Ex-Gowen Man Credited With Saving Infant's Life," *Ventura County Star* (December 16, 1992).

Chapter 5

1. "Tough Decisions in a Downturn Don't Have to Lead to Disengaged Employees," Hay Group press release (August 13, 2009), *www.haygroup.com/ww/Press/Details.aspx?ID=21404* (accessed April 6, 2011).

2. Ibid.

3. Ibid.

4. Ibid.

5. "The National Benchmark Study: Employee Motivation Affects Subsequent Stock Price," Workplace Research Foundation and University of Michigan, *http://workplaceresearchfoundation.org/index.php?option=com_content&view=article&id=47&Itemid=55* (accessed April 7, 2011).

6. Timothy Sturgeon, *Understanding Silicon Valley* (Palo Alto, Calif.: Stanford University Press, 2000).

7. Bill Walsh, Steve Jamison, and Craig Walsh, *The Score Takes Care of Itself* (New York: Portfolio, 2009).

8. Ritch K. Eich, "A competitive edge in reputation building," *Ventura County Star* (December 6, 2008).

9. Ritch K. Eich, "The St. Joe's Gala: A Benefit with A Purpose," *National Association for Hospital Development Journal* (Winter/Spring 1983).

10. Ritch K. Eich, "Giants Manager Baker Bats a Thousand in Prostate Cancer Treatment," *Stanford Report* (2002). Reprinted with permission from the Stanford Medical School's Office of Communication & Public Affairs.

11. "Johnnie B. (Dusty) Baker," Dusty Baker Baseball Camp, *www.dustybakerbaseballcamp.com/doc.asp?id=4* (accessed April 23, 2011).

12. Dr. Richard Schreiner. Interview with the author, June 8, 2011.

Chapter 6

1. Buckminster Fuller, *Critical Path* (St. Martin's Griffin Edition, 1982), 251.

2. Peter F. Drucker, *Managing The Non-Profit Organization.* (New York: Harper Paperbacks, 2006).

3. "Crotonville: The Epicenter of Learning at GE," General Electric Website, *www.ge.com/pdf/innovation/leadership/leadership_ development_fact_sheet.pdf* (accessed April 11, 2011).

4. Harold Edwards. Interview with author, May 23, 2011.

5. Ibid.

6. "Sixth Annual Hay Group Study Identifies Best Companies for Leadership," Hay Group press release (January 25, 2011), *www.haygroup.com/ww/press/Details.aspx?ID=28838* (accessed February 2, 2011).

7. Mark VanderKlipp. Interview with author, July 3, 2011.

8. "Gates Reflects on Leadership," American Forces Press Service (March 13, 2007), *www.defense.gov/pdf/Gatesinterview031307.pdf* (accessed April 11, 2011).

9. Larry Ames. Interview with author, May 8, 2011.

10. Alden B. Dow Home and Studio Tour, Midland, Michigan, July 11, 2011.

Chapter 7

1. Michael Bradbury. Interview with author, May 24, 2011.

2. David Brandon. Interview with author, May 29, 2011.

3. Ibid.

4. Ibid.

5. Michael Bradbury. Interview with author, May 24, 2011.

6. Roger Kahn, *The Boys of Summer* (New York: HarperCollins, 1987).

7. Interview with Bob Woodruff on ABC's *Nightline*, August 8, 2008.

8. David Brandon. Interview with author, May 29, 2011.

9. R.K. Goldberg, "Regaining Public Trust," *Health Affairs* (1998). See also R.K. Goldberg, "The Power of Public Relations," *Hospitals & Health Networks* (October 6, 2011).

Chapter 8

1. Marshall Loeb, et al. "What Managers Can Learn From Manager Reagan," *Fortune Magazine* (September 15, 1986).

2. Tony Zinni and Tony Koltz, *Leading the Charge: Leadership Lessons from the Battlefield to the Boardroom* (New York: Palgrave Macmillan, 2009).

3. Winston Churchill, *A Modern Chronicle: Complete.* (Middlesex, England: Echo Library, 2007).

4. Michael Bradbury. Interview with author, May 24, 2011.

5. Steve Jobs. Commencement address, Stanford University, June 12, 2005.

Bibliography

Abrashoff, D. Michael. *It's Our Ship*. New York: Business Plus, 2008.

Allen, Judy. *Event Planning*. Etobicoke, Ontario: John Wiley & Sons, 2003.

Alsop, Ron. *The Trophy Kids Grow Up*. San Francisco: Jossey-Bass, 2008.

"Armed Forces: Zinging Zumwalt, U.S.N." *Time Magazine* (November 9, 1970), *Ventura County Star*. Ventura, Calif.

Baker, William F., and Michael O'Malley. *Leading With Kindness*. New York: AMACOM, 2008.

Barner, Robert. *Bench Strength*. New York: AMACOM, 2006.

Bennis, Warren. *On Becoming a Leader*. Reading, Mass.: Addison-Wesley, 1989.

Bennis, Warren, and Burt Nanus. *Leaders*. New York: HarperCollins, 1985.

Bennis, Warren, and Robert J. Thomas. "Crucibles of Leadership." *Harvard Business Review on Developing Leaders*. Boston: Harvard Business School Press, 2004.

Benton, D. A. *How to Think Like a CEO*. New York: Warner Books, 1996.

Bergman, Barrie. *Nice Guys Finish First*. Self-published, 2009.

Betof, Ed. "Leaders as Teachers." *T+D*, (May 2004), 55–62.

Brokaw, Tom. *The Greatest Generation.* New York: Random House, 1998.

Bracey, Hyler. *Building Trust: How to Get It! How to Keep It!* Self-published, 2002.

Bryant, Adam. "He Wants Subjects, Verbs and Objects." *New York Times,* April 26, 2009.

Cannon, Jeff, and Jon Cannon. *Leadership Lessons of the Navy Seals.* New York: McGraw-Hill, 2003.

Charan, Ram. *Leadership in the Era of Economic Uncertainty.* New York: McGraw-Hill, 2009.

Choudhury, Uttara. "Wharton's Leadership Program is at the Heart of MBA Life." Braingainmag.com, July 16, 2011.

Cohen, Eli, and Noel Tichy. "How Leaders Develop Leaders." *Training & Development* (May 1997).

Collins, Jim. *Good to Great.* New York: HarperCollins, 2001.

———. *How the Mighty Fall.* New York: HarperCollins, 2009.

Conaty, Bill, and Ram Charan. *The Talent Masters.* New York: Crown Business, 2010.

Covey, Stephen M.R. *The Speed of Trust.* New York: Free Press, 2006.

Crockett, Roger O. "How P&G Finds and Keeps a Prized Workforce." *BusinessWeek* (April 9, 2009).

Deal, Terrence E., and Allen A. Kennedy. *Corporate Cultures.* Reading, Mass.: Addison-Wesley, 1982.

Denove, Chris, and James D. Power, IV. *Satisfaction.* New York: Portfolio, 2006.

DePree, Max. *Leadership Is an Art.* New York: CURRENCY, 1989.

———. *Leadership Jazz.* New York: CURRENCY, 1992.

DeVos, Rich. *Ten Powerful Phrases for Positive People*. New York: Center Street, 2008.

Drucker, Peter F. "The American CEO." *The Wall Street Journal,* December 4, 2004.

———. *The Effective Executive*. New York: HarperCollins, 2002.

———. *Managing The Non-Profit Organization*. New York: HarperCollins, 1990.

Eich, Ritch K. "Business Lessons for the Family." *Costco Connection* 26, no. 3 (2011): 15.

———. "Giants Manager Baker Bats a Thousand in Prostate Cancer Treatment." *Stanford Report*, (September 25, 2002).

———. "Leadership Wake-Up: The Millennials are Coming," *Ventura County Star* (February 21, 2010).

———. "Marching to the Beat of a Different Drum Major." *Miller McCune.com* (March 13, 2011).

———. "Your Reputation Precedes You." *Trusteeship* 14, no. 3 (2006): 13–17.

Eich, Ritch K., and William E. Wiethoff. "Toward a Model of Hierarchical Change." *Communication Quarterly* 27, no. 1 (1979): 29–37, and Taylor & Francis Group Ltd. (*www.informaworld.com*) on behalf of the Eastern Communication Association.

Erwin, Dan. *Why Is Defense Secretary Gates So Successful?* Blog, February 9, 2010. *http://danerwin.typepad.com/my_weblog/2010/02/why-is-defense-secretary-gates-success-ful.html*.

Farnham, Alan. *Forbes Great Success Stories*. New York: John Wiley & Sons, 2000.

Gagne, Matt. "A Fine Vintage." *Sports Illustrated*, February 7, 2011: 51.

Gerstner, Lewis V., Jr., *Who Says Elephants Can't Dance*. New York: HarperBusiness, 2002.

Goethals, George R., Georgia J. Sorenson, and James MacGregor Burns. *Encyclopedia of Leadership, Vols. 1–4.* Thousand Oaks, Calif.: Sage, 2004.

Goldblatt, Joe Jeff. *Special Events: Best Practices in Modern Event Management.* New York: John Wiley & Sons, 1997.

Greenleaf, Robert K. *Servant Leadership.* Mahwah, N.J.: Paulist Press, 1977.

Harari, Oren. *The Leadership Secrets of Colin Powell.* New York: McGraw-Hill, 2002.

Harvard Business Review on Developing Leaders. Boston: Harvard Business School, 2004.

Heifetz, Ronald A., Marty Linsky, and Alexander Grashow. *The Practice of Adaptive Leadership.* Boston: Harvard Business Press, 2009.

Herdt, Timm. "Ex-Gowen Man Credited With Saving Infant's Life." *Ventura County Star* (December 16, 1992).

Hesselbein, Frances, Marshall Goldsmith, and Richard Beckhard. *The Leader of the Future.* San Francisco, Calif.: Jossey-Bass, 1996.

Howard, Carole M., and Wilma K. Mathews. *On Deadline.* Prospect Heights, Ill.: Waveland Press, 2000.

Hoyle, Leonard H. *Event Marketing.* New York: John Wiley & Sons, 2002.

Iacocca, Lee. *Where Have All the Leaders Gone.* New York: Scribner, 2007.

Kahn, Roger. *The Boys of Summer.* New York: HarperCollins, 1987.

Kennedy, Caroline. *Profiles in Courage for Our Time.* New York: Hyperion, 2002.

Kennedy, Edward M. *True Compass.* New York: Twelve, 2009.

Kotter, John P. *A Sense of Urgency.* Boston: Harvard Business Press, 2008.

———. *A Force for Change.* New York: The Free Press, 1990.

Kouzes, James M., and Barry Z. Posner. *The Leadership Challenge.* San Francisco: Jossey-Bass, 2007.

Lafley, A.G., and Ram Charan. *The Game-Changer.* New York: Crown Business, 2008.

Laymon, Rob, and Kate Campbell. "Learning to Lead, Marine Style." *Wharton Alumni Magazine* (Summer 2001).

Lemons, James. "Richard L. Schreiner, M.D." Remarks, IUPUI Retiring Faculty Recognition Luncheon, Indianapolis, Indiana, (May 3, 2011).

Lucas, James R. *The Passionate Organization.* New York: AMACOM, 1999.

Maxwell, John C. *The 21 Indispensable Qualities of a Leader.* Nashville, Tenn.: Thomas Nelson, 1999.

McIlvaine, Andrew R. "GE Opens the Doors to Crotonville." *Human Resource Executive Online* (November 23, 2009).

"Nation: Humanizing the U.S. Military." *Time Magazine* (December 21, 1970).

"Old vs. New Forms of Leadership." Wisconsin Leadership Institute

Oliver, Vicky. *Bad Bosses, Crazy Co-Workers & Other Office Idiots.* Naperville, Ill.: Sourcebooks, 2008.

Orfela, Paul and Ann Marsh. *Copy This!: Lessons from a Hyperactive Dyslexic who Turned a Bright Idea Into One of America's Best Companies.* New York: Workman Publishing, 2005.

O'Reilly, Charles A., III. and Jeffrey Pfeffer. *Hiden Value: How Great Companies Achieve Extraordinary Results with Ordinary People* Boston: Harvard Business School Press, 2000.

Ornstein, Norman J. "Ted Kennedy: A Senate Giant, Partisan Hero and Legislative Master." *Roll Call* (May 21, 2008).

Pacific Coast Business Times. Santa Barbara, Calif.

Pfeffer, Jeffrey. *What Were They Thinking?* Boston: Harvard Business School Press, 2007.

Reina, Dennis S., and Michelle L. Reina. *Trust & Betrayal in the Workplace.* San Francisco, Calif.: Berrett-Koehler Publishers, Inc., 1999.

Reynolds, Cynthia Furlong. *Jiffy: A Family Tradition.* Chelsea, Mich.: Chelsea Milling Company, 2008.

Robbins, Stephen P., and Timothy A. Judge. *Organizational Behavior.* Upper Saddle River, N.J.: Pearson, 2009.

Rucker, Philip. "Kennedy's 'Farm System' Now Wields Power." *The Washington Post* (August 28, 2009).

Schembechler, Bo, and John U. Bacon. *Bo's Lasting Lessons.* New York: Business Plus, 2007.

Schwartz, Larry. "Jackie Changed Face of Sports." ESPN.com (October 10, 2002).

Senor, Dan, and Saul Singer. *A Start-up Nation.* New York: Hachette, 2009.

Sevier, Robert A. *Building a Brand That Matters.* Hiawatha, Iowa: Strategy Publishing, Inc., 2002.

———. *An Integrated Marketing Workbook.* Hiawatha, Iowa: Strategy Publishing, Inc., 2003.

———. *Thinking Outside the Box.* Hiawatha, Iowa: Strategy Publishing, Inc., 2001.

Slater, Robert. *Jack Welch & The G.E. Way.* New York: McGraw-Hill, 1999.

Sparks, Dennis. "Explain, Inspire, Lead: An Interview With Noel Tichy." *JSD* 26, no. 2 (2005).

Sutton, Robert I. *Good Boss, Bad Boss.* New York: Business Plus, 2010.

———. *The No Asshole Rule.* New York: Warner Business Books, 2007.

Thompson, William. *Gumption.* Self-published, 2010.

Tichy, Noel M., and Warren G. Bennis. *Judgment: How Winning Leaders Make Great Calls.* New York: Portfolio, 2007.

Tichy, Noel M., and Eli Cohen. "GE's Crotonville: A Staging Ground for Corporate Revolution." *The Academy of Management EXECUTIVE* III, no. 2 (1989).

———. *The Leadership Engine.* New York: Collins Business Essentials, 2007.

Vogel, Steve. "Saluting the Admiral Who Steered the Navy." *The Washington Post* (January 11, 2000), B01.

Walsh, Bill, Steve Jamison, and Craig Walsh. *The Score Takes Care of Itself.* New York: Portfolio, 2009.

Weick, Karl E., and Kathleen M. Sutcliffe. *Managing the Unexpected.* San Francisco, Calif.: Jossey-Bass, 2001.

Weiss, Alan. *"Good Enough" Isn't Enough...: Nine Challenges for Companies That Choose to Be Great.* New York: AMACOM, 2000.

Weiss, Kenneth R. "No Longer the University of Second Choice." *Los Angeles Times Magazine* (September 17, 2000).

Welch, Jack. *Winning.* New York: HarperCollins, 2005.

Whitehead, Don. *The Dow Story.* New York: McGraw-Hill, 1968.

Woodall, Marian, K. *Thinking on Your Feet.* Bend, Oreg.: PBC, 1996.

Zenger, John H., and Joseph Folkman. *The Extraordinary Leader.* New York: McGraw-Hill, 2002.

Helpful Websites and Blogs

Aaker on Brands (*www.prophet.com/blog/aakeronbrands*): A blog from David Aaker, recognized authority on brands, and vice chairman of Prophet, global strategic brand and marketing consultants.

Eich Associated (*www.eichassociated.com*): Strategic branding, marketing and communications, and management coaching firm headed by author Ritch K. Eich.

Harvard Business Review Blog Network (*http://blogs.hbr.org*): A series of blogs from all kinds of business, management, and leadership experts, along with others.

Hay Group (*www.haygroup.com/ww/Index.aspx*): Global management consulting firm with lots of useful information on leadership, management, business strategies, and more.

Leadership At Work/Harvard Business Review (*http://blogs. hbr.org/baldoni/*): A blog by John Baldoni, leadership expert, consultant, author, and executive coach; more blogs from Baldoni at *www.johnbaldoni.com*.

McKinsey Quarterly (*https://www.mckinseyquarterly.com/ home.aspx*): An online business journal of business management strategy articles, surveys, and interviews from global business management and consultants, McKinsey & Company.

Seth's Blog (*http://sethgodin.typepad.com/*): A blog from Seth Godin, top-selling author, marketing expert, and leadership guru.

Work Matters (*http://bobsutton.typepad.com/*): A blog by Robert (Bob) Sutton, professor of management science and engineering at Stanford University, and an expert on the psychology of business and management.

Index

About the Author

Ritch K. Eich, PhD, is a nationally recognized marketing, branding, public relations, and leadership practitioner with more than 30 years of executive success. His business experience spans some of the "best and brightest" organizations in the for-profit and non-profit sectors in hospitals, agriculture, higher education, health insurance, and government. Ritch has led marketing, branding, and communications divisions at such premier institutions as Stanford University Medical Center, Blue Shield of California, and Indiana University Medical Center. Ritch has held key recruiting, business development, and fundraising positions at Pomona College, St. Joseph Mercy Hospital System, and the University of Michigan. More recently, he spearheaded the highly successful branding initiative at California Lutheran University during his six years as their first vice president of marketing.

The author of numerous publications, public papers, opinion pieces, and convention presentations, Ritch's efforts have been recognized by the Council for the Advancement and Support of Education (CASE), Strategic Healthcare Marketing, the Association of American Medical Colleges (AAMC), the U.S Navy and Marine Corps, the U.S. Senate, HERMES awards, the international MarCom Awards organization, and other professional associations.

Ritch was elected to the board of directors of the University of Michigan Alumni Association, an independent organization that serves approximately 500,000 alumni and friends of the university. He was also selected to join the boards of directors of the Santa Barbara and Ventura Colleges of Law and the Kingsmen Shakespeare Festival. He is a past chair of the board of trustees of Los Robles Hospital and Medical Center and is also a past member of Rotary and United Way. Ritch was also a Pharmaceutical Research and Manufacturers Association Fellow at Abbott Laboratories in Chicago. He served on the founding board of trustees of the University of California–Merced Foundation, on the founding boards of directors for the Ronald McDonald House of West Michigan and the USS Indianapolis Memorial. Ritch also served on the board of VCEDA (Ventura County Economic Development Association) and the University of Michigan Military ROTC Board, and he is a graduate of Leadership San Francisco and Stanley K. Lacy's Executive Leadership Association's Opportunity Indianapolis.

He has served on military academies' selection committees for U.S. Senators from Michigan and Indiana. Ritch achieved the rank of Captain, U.S. Naval Reserve, and has served in the Pentagon, the Joint Chiefs of Staff, NATO, the Pacific and Atlantic fleets, as well as other joint commands.

He is married to the former Joan Taylor Cummings of Greenville, Michigan. They have two sons, Geoff and Ted, who graduated with academic honors from the U.S. Naval Academy and Vanderbilt University, respectively. Geoff, a former Marine Harrier pilot who flew combat missions in both Iraq and Afghanistan, is an executive director at Amgen, Inc. in Thousand Oaks, California. Ted, who served two tours in the Persian Gulf enforcing UN sanctions against Iraq and subsequently during Operation Enduring Freedom, is an attorney with Hogan Lovells in Washington, D.C.

Ritch believes it is a leader's reponsibilty to share his expetise and experience with others, and has served in a voluntary leadership position at the following organizations:

USS Indianpolis *Memorial. Photo by Joan Taylor Cummings Eich.*

KCLU-FM (NPR) Studios. Photo by Erik Hagen/
California Luthern University.

Western Michigan Ronald McDonald House. Photo by Craig VanDerLende/Ronald McDonald House of Western Michigan.

The University Of California–Merced. Photo by UC Merced Office of Communications.

United States Navy Memorial, Washington, D.C. All Rights Reserved. Used with the permission of the United States Navy Memorial Foundation (www.navymemorial.org).